Stairway to Heaven

Selected Sermons by
Rabbi Elliot J. Cosgrove

Stairway to Heaven

Selected Sermons by
Rabbi Elliot J. Cosgrove

2014–2015 / 5775

ParkAvenue
Synagogue ק"ק אגודת ישרים

Stairway to Heaven: Selected Sermons by Rabbi Elliot J. Cosgrove
2014-2015 / 5775

Copyright 2015 Park Avenue Synagogue

ISBN 978-0-9897672-3-1

Printed in the United States of America in 2015

Park Avenue Synagogue
50 East 87th Street
New York, NY 10128
www.pasyn.org

Contents

Foreword

This seventh volume of Rabbi Cosgrove's sermons takes its title, *Stairway to Heaven*, from the seventh parashah of the Torah, Va-yetzei. In this parashah Jacob leaves home, and reading through the sermons of Rabbi Cosgrove's seventh year at Park Avenue Synagogue, we see that his topics spanned the world, from our home in New York City to the Mideast. The summer 2014 war in Gaza, European anti-Semitism, terrorism, the US/Israel relationship, and internal Israeli policies and politics were all examined on our bimah and related to our weekly Torah reading. More than any year since Rabbi Cosgrove came to Park Avenue Synagogue, he drew our focus to the world beyond our community.

This volume begins with sermons inspired by the book of Deuteronomy; "Abnormal Evil" relates the biblical figure Amalek to the Hamas firing of rockets on Israeli civilians and other atrocities around the world and calls us to "[rouse] our world from its slumber." Soon afterwards, in his Rosh Hashanah sermon "The 615th Commandment," the rabbi's poignant, deeply personal story of the anti-Semitic attack on his young cousins in England twenty years ago set the stage for a message of staunch support of Israel in a world questioning Israel's actions in Gaza.

The rabbi's focus then turned to Europe. In "Vive La France?" Rabbi Cosgrove spoke on the need for standing shoulder-to-shoulder in solidarity with European Jews. After terrorist attacks in France around the time of Purim, the sermon "European Jewry: Stay or Go?" connected the challenge of standing up to present-day circumstances in Europe with the story of Esther.

Next, Israeli/US relations and Israel politics and policies came to the forefront. In "A Time to Stand Down, Not Double Down," Rabbi Cosgrove commented on Israeli Prime Minister Bibi Netanyahu's controversial address to Congress and its potential damage to the Israel/US relationship, and on the treatment of non-Orthodox Judaism in Israel, and he called for a "dialed down" tone. "The Hidden Question" covered Israel's relationship with her Palestinian Arab neighbors, and "Destiny Knocking," a sermon for Yom HaAtzma'ut, called for Park Avenue Synagogue "to demonstrate to the world that one can defend Israel in the public sphere, advocate for a two-state solution, and work towards a pluralistic vision of global Jewish peoplehood." Finally, "Two Worlds of Judaism" illuminated the differences between the religious leanings of the newly elected Israeli government and the direction in which American Jewry is headed, seeking to encourage dialogue and partnership.

Other insightful sermons this past year included "Attitude of Gratitude," which is one that any synagogue leader could use to inspire members to be charitable, as "gratitude and giving go hand-in-hand." Rabbi Cosgrove's Yom Kippur sermon about Rabbi Milton Steinberg's most famous book, *As a Driven Leaf*, reminded members that no matter what, "there is still comfort, solace, and support to be found in community." "Towers to the Heavens" inspired us to "not think about what we don't have, but what we do have . . . and be satisfied with it," while "I Will Be What I Will Be" encourages us "to build a community that supports each other in times of need, that treats every human being as equal in the eyes of God."

Rabbi Cosgrove wrapped up his seventh year at Park Avenue Synagogue by bringing external and internal issues together. In "The Best Defense" he welcomed Israeli statesman Yair Lapid, who advocates for a pluralistic vision of Jewish life in Israel while pointing out to our community that the best thing we can do to support that pluralistic vision is "by living vibrant and engaged Jewish lives, by building dynamic Jewish communities that dare not be ignored."

All of these sermons are fantastic reading. They have even more impact when you hear them live in the sanctuary. I encourage you to join us for Shabbat services when our clergy team blends meaningful sermons together with prayer and inspiring music to engage us each week. Our combination of tradition and innovation continues to address the needs of our community. I hope to see you on Shabbat.

B'shalom,
Art Penn
Chairman of the Board

Preface

The title of this volume comes both from Jacob's nocturnal vision described in Genesis 28:12 and also from the greatest rock 'n' roll song ever written. I cannot think of a better title for a book of sermons and anthem for my life as a congregational rabbi.

The longer I serve as a congregational rabbi, the more convinced I become that a synagogue is the most countercultural institution in the landscape of American life. In any context, the notion of "membership" implies a cognitive leap into an institution, community, tribe, and tradition particular to a certain group; in the case of the synagogue, that group is the Jews. As the recent Pew study made clear, American Jewry is no longer the homogenous community it may have once been. The emergence of all sorts of hyphenated and blended identities has blurred the boundary lines of our increasingly textured and diverse Jewish family. What is the message and mission of our so very parochial institution in a world that puts such a premium on the universal?

Do we, one may ask, really need synagogues to live Jewishly? In an era of disintermediation, who is to say that synagogues won't go the way of Blockbuster Video and Borders Books? It is no longer necessary to join a synagogue to have clergy present at your "matchings, hatchings, and dispatchings." In our free-market world, one need not make the emotionally cumbersome and financially significant investment in a synagogue in order to have a rabbi officiate at your family simcha or sorrow. After all, if one can "be Jewish" on one's own terms, without making the commitment to Hebrew School – why not do it? Just how important is Jewish literacy anyway? Isn't it just a matter of time before Jewish education feels the same pinch as liberal arts on the college campus? Given the competing demands on my child's attention and schedule, am I really expected to prioritize the non-marketable skills of Jewish literacy and *menschlichkeit*? Does a prayer service really need to last three hours? Both the opera and Major League Baseball are adapting to the economics of diminishing attention spans – isn't it time that synagogues do the same?

At the core of the challenge sits not just the countercultural nature of the synagogue, but the enterprise of Jewish life and living upon which every synagogue is based. Perhaps more than any other faith, Judaism is a religion that asks its adherents to participate in a system of responsibilities, commitments, and obligations. To be Jewish is to suggest that one should belong in a certain way, behave in a certain way, and believe in a certain way. Our ritual observances and mitzvot, our festival cycle, our prayer book, our sacred texts all signal a system that has expectations of us, even if, perhaps especially if, they are not convenient. Jewish authenticity has never been contingent on Judaism being done "your way." And here lies the rub. In our world of hyper-individualism, are we willing to allow for the possibility that our tradition, our community, and our God have expectations of us, expectations that may run counter to our whims and desires? Can a synagogue – whose very mission is founded on these demanding assumptions at the heart of our faith – withstand the countervailing forces of our time?

To all of these observations and challenges, I have but one answer: Exactly and absolutely.

The future of the synagogue, and by extension, American Jewish life, will not come by way of mimicking the dominant cultural forces of our day. Only by appreciating and embracing the differentiated and unique role of a synagogue in the lives of its members will we serve and preserve the Jewish future. Regardless of the technological innovations on the horizon, there can never be a substitute for face-to-face dialogue. No online community will ever replace a congregation of souls in communion with one another. Since the Garden of Eden, every creature has understood that his or her existential loneliness can only be redressed by the presence of another. The root of "synagogue" is the Greek word meaning "assembly." To assemble in common cause with individuals and families of different ages and at different stages of life in order to address matters of ultimate importance – over the course of our lifetime and perhaps through generations – is a role that only a synagogue can claim. Rooms can be rented and clergy can be hired, but only by way of the relationships built in a synagogue community, compounded over a lifetime of joys and sorrows, is the meaning of synagogue life rendered evident. Past, present and future, it is the communal nature of our enterprise that is our strength.

As for the parochial nature of a synagogue, we must indeed be aware that the nature of American Jewry has changed. Our synagogue must adapt to the reality that an increasing percentage of our congregational family may not have been born as Jews. This acknowledgement, however, only forces us to sharpen the argument of "Why be Jewish?" to the benefit of the entire community. Notwithstanding the power of "from generation to generation," our age must construct a compelling rationale for living an engaged Jewish life. Why would anyone opt to live Jewishly? How shall we articulate a persuasive language of Jewish identity that does not suffer from the triumphalism or exclusionism of the past? How exactly shall the Jewish community prompt our children towards endogamy *and* ensure that our future sons- and daughters-in-law, if born of non-Jewish families, regard themselves as full participants in the Jewish future? There are no easy answers to these questions, but it is these questions and not the questions of a bygone era to which our synagogue must be committed. Unlike other generations, the assimilation of our era does not signal rejection of Jewish identity – rather unfamiliarity with the tools for positively expressing Jewish identity. Even the most peripheral soul seeks to connect to a tradition and a people that long preceded our existence and, please God, will extend well after our time here on earth.

In the years ahead, our synagogue will undertake a constant process of reimagining itself. The length of prayer services, the modalities of educating our children, and the boundaries of Jewish identity will all come under scrutiny, to name but a few of the necessary conversations on the Jewish communal docket. Substantive as these changes may be, they do not signal a change from our core mission of seeking to inspire, educate, and support our membership towards living passion-filled Jewish lives. Religion – good religion – is not a vending machine that delivers results with a push of the button. Judaism takes time. Judaism asks us to appreciate a Shabbat dinner, a Passover seder, the beauty of the cantor's voice, waiting between meat and milk, studying our tradition, and enjoying the blessing of a community that has developed over time. Synagogues, like any stairway to heaven, ask us to climb higher and longer than we otherwise would. Contrary to our world that demands everything instantly, a spiritual life acknowledges that the answers may not come quickly and sometimes they don't come at all. That is a good thing.

The Jewish future will be determined by the degree to which we are able to identify those elements of our tradition that should be maintained – the ones that distinguish us from the dominant culture of our day, thus securing our differentiated mission – versus those elements that need to be retooled in order to serve the needs of the present and future generations. It is a difficult task that will extend far into the years ahead. I invite you to help shape that conversation. To paraphrase the popular prayer, perhaps at this time we should ask God for the resolve to embrace the things we should not change, the courage to change the things we can, and the wisdom to know the difference between the two.

I hope that the sermons in this volume are a step in the right direction. If, as a preacher of old once reflected, the role of religion is to comfort the afflicted and afflict the comfortable, then I hope that my sermons have succeeded in that task. Not to validate the long-held views of the listener, nor to offer definitive conclusions, but to respectfully and provocatively lead a communal conversation on the issues of the day. I am grateful to serve a community with such high demands of its leadership and I hope this volume (and the ones to follow) will continue to position our synagogue as the place where important conversations facing the Jewish people take place and are acted upon.

To our chairman, Art Penn, I thank you and our entire lay leadership for your tireless commitment to our communal well-being. Thank you to Jean Bloch Rosensaft and to Rebecca Raphael Feuerstein for the many hours you have invested in the editorial process. Finally, to my colleague, copy editor, and conscience, Marga Hirsch: I thank you for everything you do towards the production of this volume.

Every year at this time I have the opportunity to identify a relative, teacher, or mentor to whom I will dedicate a volume of sermons – an individual without whom I would not be who I am today. As I enter the second seven-year cycle of my tenure at Park Avenue Synagogue, it strikes me as altogether appropriate to give thanks to two individuals without whom I would not hold the position I do. Geoffrey Colvin and Amy Bressman, both distinguished past chairmen of our community, were "the ones who hired me." Amy, then chairman, and Geoff, together with his devoted search committee, guided me and the community into an exciting new chapter of congregational history. They and their families have been a continuing source of guidance, friendship, and support every step of the way. Amy and Geoff, I love my job, and more importantly, my wife and children love our life. I hope that my service to the community you love so much continues to meet your highest hopes, and that you and your beautiful families know only joy in the years ahead. Please accept the dedication of this volume as a small gesture towards repaying my incalculable debt of gratitude to you both.

Elliot J. Cosgrove
July 21, 2015
5 Av 5775

Ki Tetzei
Abnormal Evil

Resting in a book review in this week's *New York Times* is a question whose origins can be traced to the beginning of time and the inner reaches of the human soul. "Does absolute evil exist?" The book in review, by Bettina Stangneth, is called *Eichmann Before Jerusalem: The Unexamined Life of a Mass Murderer*. The title is a conscious reference to Hannah Arendt's infamous 1963 book *Eichmann in Jerusalem: A Report on the Banality of Evil*. Adolf Eichmann was the chief of the Jewish Department of the Gestapo during World War II and one of the architects of the Final Solution aimed at the extermination of European Jewry. When Eichmann was brought to justice by Israel in the early 1960s, his public trial played a cathartic role for a post-Holocaust Israeli and worldwide Jewish community, transformed from the persecuted to the prosecutor. The proceedings of the trial were documented in Arendt's book. Its subtitle – *A Report on the Banality of Evil* – signals one of her most controversial and contested claims. In brief, Arendt characterizes Eichmann not as a sociopathic sadist, but rather, as an unthinking bureaucrat, an amoral individual who was just carrying out orders. In her estimation, Eichmann was not a "monster," but a "clown." Arendt did not soft pedal the cruel nature of Eichmann's deeds, but by her characterizing them (and him) as ordinary or banal, his evil became unexceptional, a claim which in a post-Holocaust context was and remains altogether controversial. (NYT, September 2, 2014)

Stangneth's new book makes her the latest in a long line of scholars who take issue with Arendt's thesis. For Stangneth, Eichmann was anything but a mindless functionary. In revealing Eichmann's notes and writings before his trial in Jerusalem, she demonstrates that Eichmann was a man of great intellectual sophistication. He was fully aware of his deeds, a willful, conscious actor who "dispatched, decreed, allowed, took steps, issued orders and gave audiences." (p. 18) His actions and his deeds were anything but banal; his evil was absolute and thus altogether extraordinary. Neither the execution of Eichmann nor, for that matter, the execution of any single individual would or could bring justice to the victims of the Shoah. Nevertheless, once Eichmann's deeds are named for the diabolical evil that they were, his execution may be seen as a step towards fulfilling our obligation to eradicate evil in this wounded world in which we live.

The Arendt-Stangneth debate is not only philosophical, but also of tremendous practical import. In an article on religion and international human rights, the philosopher Michael Wyschograd wrote that "From time to time, evils appear on the world scene which are in a class unto themselves. These are instances of large-scale, premeditated murder of large numbers of human beings in systematic ways." Among the cases of such abnormal evil, Wyschograd lists World War I, the Soviet Gulag System and, of course, the Holocaust. The essay, which is worth reading in its entirety, goes to great lengths to acknowledge the prickly nature of one or more states deciding to interfere in the domestic affairs of another sovereign state. Nevertheless, Wyschograd concludes, "In the face of abnormal evil, abnormal responses are necessary." As the book of Leviticus commands: "Do not stand by idly by the blood of your brother." "There comes a point," writes Wyschograd, "when military intervention is justified and the religious community has a duty to speak clearly when that point is reached." (*Formation of Social Policy in the Jewish and Catholic Traditions*, pp. 136-139)

Which brings us back to the question with which we began. Does absolute evil exist? How does absolute evil differ from everyday evil? Would we know abnormal evil if we saw it? Because if we did, if we lived in a time of radical or abnormal evil, then it is not only permissible, but it is our obligation to wipe it out. To be fair, we must acknowledge that the opposite might also be true. Maybe evil, like a lot of things, is merely in the eye of the beholder. "One man's terrorist," as the expression goes, "is another man's freedom fighter." One could argue that great powers, America included, assign moral labels – good, evil, abnormally evil – not on absolute terms, but on the basis of interests being protected. Is it really such a coincidence, to paraphrase Wyschograd, that we rarely, if ever, conclude something to be evil if doing so serves against our interests? Our world is a relative one, full of moral equivalences. Everyone has a point of view and every action exists in a broader context that may justify the seemingly unjustified. Who are we to have the audacity to declare anyone or anything absolutely evil, especially when doing so may call on us and others to make great sacrifices as a country?

As Jews, not only do we believe that such evil can exist in this world, but we have a word for it, and that word is *Amalek*. Our Torah reading states: "Remember what Amalek did to you as you came forth out of Egypt; how he met you on the way, and cut down all the stragglers at your rear, when you were faint and weary; and he feared not God." Therefore, the text continues, "you shall blot the remembrance of Amalek from under the heaven; you shall not forget." (Deuteronomy 25:17–19)

Amalek's genealogy traces back to his grandfather Esau. Unlike other clans with whom the Israelites battled over territories or otherwise, the Amalekites engaged in a war of killing non-combatants. In his study on the topic, Avi Sagi explains that Amalek "transgressed every norm of a just war." Not only did they have no cause for going to war, but they waged the war against the most fragile, the ones in the rear, behind the army. (*Harvard Theological Review* 87:3, 1994) At the heart of their sin, explains Nechama Leibowitz, is that "they feared not God," a condemnatory descriptor assigned to no other people but Amalek. As Jews, our love for humanity is tied directly to our relationship to God. All human beings – old/young, Jew/gentile, rich/poor, gay/straight, tall/short, even our foes – are deserving of respect because we are all, equally, created in the image of God. Conversely, as in the case of Amalek, to not fear God signals the inability to acknowledge the divine and common spark embedded in all of humanity. Such people, to adopt Wyschograd's language, are abnormally evil, and it is our obligation to eradicate that evil from our midst.

Ever since, in every generation, our people have been eyes wide open to the emergence of Amalek. In the biblical and rabbinic tradition, the pedigrees of those who have persecuted Israel – Agag, Haman, Rome, and others – all trace back to Amalek. But even where there is no direct lineage, as Jews we are forewarned of the ever-present possibility for Amalek-like behavior, what Zev Garber calls *amalekut*. To live by the sword, to slaughter innocents, this is *amalekut* (*Jewish Bible Theology*, pp. 147-159). Not just literally, but metaphysically, *amalekut* came to represent any past or current forms of extreme dehumanization. Be it in the name of nationalism, radical religion or any other cause, that is evil: That is *amalekut*.

Yes, I do believe that we live in an age where once again the seeds of Amalek have taken root. The tragic death and destruction in Gaza does not mitigate the evil intentions of Hamas: a charter unambiguously calling for the destruction of the Jewish state. The indiscriminate firing on civilian populations, tunnels dug for the sole purpose of abducting and murdering Israelis – this is *amalekut*! And were it to be the case that Israel, or any friend of Israel, demonstrated such an abject disrespect for human life, then war must be waged against the "Amalek" within. As my friend and colleague Danny Gordis has written, the Jewish community must dispense with its timidity and learn to call its enemies out for who they are. (*The Jerusalem Post*, July 17, 2014) I pray for the day when Israel and her enemies turn their swords into plowshares, but until that day, Israel has every right to defend herself against those who would seek her destruction.

As other events on the world stage continue to develop daily – in Iraq, in Syria, creeping into Jordan and right up to borders of the Golan Heights – I am struck again and again that we are living through a period of *amalekut*: mass murder, the slaughter of innocents, and grotesque beheadings and public executions. Not every wrong falls in the class of abnormal evil. We need not look far back in our own country's history to recall times when the label of evil has proven to be a self-serving abuse of the term. It might not be in our short- or long-term interests, but evil it is and if only half of what we are reading and seeing is true, then there is little doubt that our era is seeing Amalek's latest incarnation. As the Israeli author and peacenik Amos Oz recently reminded us, in 1945 the lives of those in Theresienstadt were saved not by peace demonstrators with placards and flowers, but by soldiers and submachine guns. Lest we forget, we are the people of "never again," even when – especially when – the lives in question are people who are strangers to us and our direct interests.

Tolstoy once wrote: "There are no conditions of life to which a man cannot get accustomed, especially if he sees them accepted by everyone around him." (*Anna Karenina*) It is far too easy to let evil become banal or ordinary, to allow ourselves to be lulled into a world of moral equivalences and willed inertia. As Jews, as human beings, as lovers of humanity, we must protect that humanity, never ever permitting ourselves to grow accustomed to acts of sheer diabolical evil. We must be vigilant, we must be responsive, and most of all, as a religious community it is our responsibility to announce the arrival of abnormal evil when we see it – thus rousing our world from its slumber.

Ki Tavo
Attitude of Gratitude

I have no idea if Wharton Business School Professor Adam Grant is familiar with rabbinic literature, but I suspect the author of the bestselling book *Give and Take* would enjoy reading the fifth chapter of *Pirkei Avot*, The Ethics of the Fathers. Chapter 5, mishnah 10 states:

> There are four character types among people. One who says, "What's mine is mine and what's yours is yours." This is the average type. One who says, "What's mine is yours and what's yours is mine." This person is an ignoramus. One who says, "What's mine is yours and what's yours is yours." This person is pious. And finally, one who says, "What's yours is mine and what's mine is mine." This person is wicked.

The passage divides humanity into four different types of givers and takers, not just in terms of money, but by how one comports oneself in business, interpersonal relations and all manner of human interaction. Resources come in a variety of forms; money is only the most obvious one. There is wisdom; there is social capital; there is property; there is trust; and arguably our most precious commodity of all is time. But no matter what the commodity or "stuff" may be, the one thing they all have in common is their finite nature. Some stuff is mine, some stuff is yours, and a good measuring rod of who each of us is, is the degree to which and the manner by which we give, or take, of our resources. To give a person ten minutes of your time, ten dollars from your wallet, to pick up the phone on another's behalf – these are all gestures that serve as windows into our character. So, too, to take advantage of someone's trust, to take that which is not yours, to abuse another person's time – these are also indicators of who we really are. It is neither possible, nor advisable, as the rabbis understood, to give too freely of our limited resources. Nevertheless, we also know, as did the rabbis, of the distasteful disposition of the person who is unwilling or begrudging in being forthcoming with any of the "stuff" that is theirs to give.

Adam Grant divides the world not by rabbinic typologies but according to categories he has identified through years of social science research. In brief, there are "takers," there are "matchers," and there are "givers." Takers are the dog-eat-dog types, people who compete, self-promote, and first and foremost look out for themselves. Takers are marked by a sense of entitlement: What they have is their due, and what they don't have they also deserve. They are people driven not by what they give, but by what they get. Matchers are slightly different and a bit more commonplace: These are people who live according to a tit-for-tat sensibility. If they help someone, it is in order to receive something in return; favors are to be exchanged, every good deed is contingent on reciprocity, everything must be matched.

The third category, the one that the book is actually about, is the category of givers. Whether it is money, time, counsel, or connections, a giver strives to be generous for the benefit of all those around. Not only do givers give without an expectation of reciprocity, but their giving may come at some personal cost. What really interests Grant, however, is not just understanding the "giving" personality, but tracking the happiness of people who give. There are, to be sure, unhealthy types of giving – people who give so much of their resources that, like Shel Silverstein's Giving Tree, they do so to their own detriment. Such a giver suffers from burnout, fatigue, and feeling like a doormat to the world.

But there is also another category of giver, a giver who insists that the choice between "what is mine," and "what is yours" is not either/or, but both/and. Grant studies volunteers who enjoy higher levels of happiness, self-esteem, and life satisfaction because they give of their time and wisdom. Charitable individuals who work harder, longer, and smarter because they are generous with their resources.

Such individuals carry themselves with a certain spiritual posture. They are eyes wide open to the blessings of their lives; they know themselves to be fortunate; they live with an attitude of gratitude that is leveraged in the most obvious way: They give. They then see the impact their giving has on their world, and they thrive further because of it. For such people, gratitude and giving go hand-in-hand. Altruism and self-interest are not only not at odds, but they are interdependent, two sides of the same coin. One gives because one is grateful; one is grateful because one can give. It is a virtuous cycle that goes on and on and on.

Adam Grant's thesis is not exactly new, at least to the Jewish community. As far back as the opening lines of this week's Torah reading, the Jewish world has drawn a correlation between gratitude and giving. "When you enter the land," our Torah reading states, "you shall take of the first fruits of the soil and offer them before the Lord." The ancient pilgrim was obligated to recite Israel's journey from the sorrows of Egyptian oppression to freedom by way of God's saving hand; from the wilderness travail to the land of milk and honey. The basket of fruit shall be left before the Lord, and "you shall enjoy, together with the Levite and the stranger in your midst, all the bounty that the Lord your God has bestowed upon you and your household." (Deuteronomy 26:1-11)

All of the ingredients are present. The pilgrim gives from the very best, the first fruits of the harvest. The ritualized telling of Israel's spiritual and physical journey affirms that whatever the present blessings being enjoyed, they came by way of those who came before. Filled with an attitude of gratitude, two things happen to the Israelite. First, giving, and second, enjoyment. *V'samaḥta b'khol ha-tov asher natan l'kha Adonai Elohekha.* "You shall enjoy . . . all the bounty that the Lord your God has bestowed upon you." The fruits of one's labors become that much sweeter because they are shared with the Levite and the stranger. It is not either/or, it is both/and. There is gratitude, there is giving, there is enjoyment.

If there is one sentiment that Judaism seeks to engender, it is a feeling of gratitude. It is so easy to walk through this world with a glass-half-empty mentality. We wait for the other shoe to drop, suspicious of everyone and everything. Our world is so rife with hurt and imperfection that each one of us, if we chose to do so, could carry a perpetually wounded sensibility, a sensibility whose natural extension is a posture of entitlement, a posture whose natural response is to be a taker. We have been hurt, we will be hurt again, and therefore we must take what is our due, and God help the person who dares tell us otherwise.

Not so, teaches our faith. The first word a Jew utters every day is *modeh*, from the same root as *todah*: *Modeh ani l'fanekha*, grateful am I for the blessing of being alive to see a new day. The order of the words, as my classmate Rabbi Shai Held has taught, is instructive. One cannot acknowledge the self – the *ani*, I – until one has first said *modeh*, thanks. Upon entering a house of prayer we recite *mah tovu ohalekha*, "How goodly are your tents." Every prayer service contains words of *hoda'ah*/thanksgiving; every meal is followed by grace after meals. Jews have a blessing for every aspect of human existence; a spiritual regimen whose goal is to ensure we never ever become dulled to the gifts of our lives. It is not that we are unaware of the underbelly of existence and the dark side of humanity. Of course we are. But we stand firm with an attitude of gratitude: thankful to each other, thankful to God for all the good that surrounds us each day.

Like many here, I will forever remember the feeling of getting my first paycheck as a professional, in my case as an assistant rabbi in Chicago. Growing up, I knew that a generation prior, when my father received his first paycheck as a physician, he wrote it over to his father as a gesture of gratitude, just as his father had done for his parents before him. So when my turn came along, I received that paycheck, signed the back of it, and sent it home to my folks. All things being equal, I imagine my parents weren't banking on me entering the not-for-profit world, an option that I often remind my children is not for everyone. Nevertheless, the cycle of gratitude and giving was in motion. A few weeks later, I received an envelope back from my dad to discover that he had divided up that check to open up bank accounts for my children, his grandchildren.

All of us should aspire to be givers. No institution does or should rely on me to make their budget; that said, Debbie and I are proud of what we can do. But if, by virtue of my station in life, I can pick up the phone on someone's behalf, give what wisdom, time, and social capital I have to help someone along the way, I always do. And when I do, to this day I have never regretted making that effort. In fact, I am always strengthened and renewed by having stretched to make this world of ours a bit better by dint of my contribution, and I am grateful for the opportunity to do so.

In just a few weeks, we will stand together as a community on Rosh Hashanah to chant the well-known *Unetaneh Tokef* – a prayer that reminds us of God's judgment and our three primary obligations this holiday season. First, *teshuvah*, to repent and reconcile one with another. Second, *tefillah*, to pray to God with sincerity and devotion. The third activity, *tzedakah*, to give, does not make immediate sense. What does the act of giving have to do with the message of these days of judgment? The answer, I believe, lies in an attitude of gratitude. The spiritual accounting of our year gone by is not measured merely by a punch list of our deeds, of rights and wrongs committed. Our year is also measured according to the degree to which we transcend the quotidian burdens of existence and open our eyes to the beauty, goodness and good fortune of our lives; and yes, our success in doing so is signaled by our having a spiritual posture of giving. In simpler terms, it is the act of giving that announces to God and to the world that we are indeed thankful for the blessings of our lives and thus stand ready to enter the year to come.

Some people give time; others, money; others, wisdom; and others, their good name. Nobody but you can determine what resources you give and how you choose to do so, and we should all think twice before making judgments about the private choices others make. But if you want an exercise in self-inventory this holiday season, you don't need to look further than your own deeds: They are the truest windows into our souls. There is so much in this world for which to be grateful. Whether we choose to see that goodness, be grateful for it, and act on it, that is a choice that belongs to nobody in this world but you.

Erev Rosh Hashanah
With God's Love We Forgive

Once upon a time, in a small shtetl in the Pale of Settlement, there lived two young women of marrying age. Two promising men from a neighboring village were identified, arrangements were made, and the town began to prepare for the upcoming double simcha. Disaster struck when a band of marauders attacked the would-be grooms on the way to the shtetl, and one of them, tragically, was killed. The remaining groom arrived the next day and was met by the two eagerly awaiting families. The groom had no idea to which bride he was betrothed, and a fight broke out between the prospective mothers-in-law, each one pulling an arm and insisting that the young man was her daughter's intended.

The rabbi was summoned, assessed the situation, and turned to his books for wisdom. He explained that as nobody actually knew with certainty to whom the surviving suitor was betrothed, there stood no other option other than the precedent set by King Solomon: The young man must be cut in half – each bride to receive an equal share.

Upon hearing the verdict, the first mother cries out: "Rabbi, haven't we known enough suffering? God forbid any harm should befall this young man!"

To which the second mother replies: "Nu – so cut him in half – it is the only fair way to do it."

At which point the rabbi looks up at her and says, "Aha, you must be the true mother-in-law!"

Shanah tovah! To each and everyone one of you – a year of health, joy, and laughter. To the members of the Park Avenue Synagogue family, to my clergy and professional colleagues, to the lay leadership, to my mother-in-law, to Debbie's mother-in-law – may this year be filled with only the very best for you, the Jewish people and all of humanity.

Not everyone is a parent, and not everyone is blessed to have the mother and mother-in-law that I have, but there is something about the jokes Jews share about parents and their children that we all understand cuts to the core of who we are as a people – our hopes, our joys, our anxieties, and beyond. "How many Jewish mothers does it take to change a light bulb? . . . Forget it, I am fine sitting in the dark." A distinctive extract drawn from the Jewish soul: neurotic pride in our offspring distilled through a willingness to suffer the sins of the children whom we adore. Like Eskimos and snow, Jews have more words and more jokes to contend with the charged condition of parent-child relationships than we can count. To *kvell* or not to *kvell* – that is the Jewish question. It is the presence or absence of our people's most valued resource, *naches* – that is the truest window to the condition of our lives.

This evening, as we celebrate Rosh Hashanah and usher in a new year, it is extract, whose origins date back to creation itself, that we will drink. You see, Sholom Aleichem was not entirely correct when he wrote: "Adam was the luckiest man to ever live, because he had no mother-in-law." Neither Adam nor Eve may have had a mother-in-law or a mother or father to contend with, but they most certainly lived in the shadow of a rather daunting parental figure: God. Contrary to what we will recite tomorrow – *hayom harat olam*, "today the world was created," – according to the Midrash, today, Rosh Hashanah, is *not* actually the first day of creation. Rather, in the words of Rabbi Eliezer, creation began some six days ago – on the twenty-fifth of the Hebrew month of Elul. Each day creation proceeded, culminating in the first day of Tishrei, the day Adam and Eve were created, the day Adam and Eve sinned, and significantly, the day their sin was forgiven or at least mitigated by God. Today is known as *Yom ha-Din*, the Day of Judgment, because it was on this very day, the first day of the seventh month, that Adam and Eve stood in judgment in the presence of the divine, were found guilty, and were pardoned.

All biblically based religions draw on the story of Eden, but for Jews our focus is not on the original sin, but on the original *pardon* –

on God's ability, from the very beginning, to judge humanity with compassion, to see past our failings and forgive us as a parent would a child. Like Adam and Eve, we know that in the past year, we have fallen short of our God-given potential. We know that we have stumbled, and so we call on God to be merciful unto us, *k'raḥem av al banim* – as a father shows mercy to his children. Were it to be the case that God judged humanity according to a strict application of justice, we know we would not pass the test; we would not be written into the Book of Life. And so we cry out to God as a child to a parent – *Avinu Malkeinu*, "Our Father, our King." Even when – especially when – we stand exposed in our foibles, when we know we are deserving of rebuke, we beg God to remember that in God's eyes we are *ha-ben yakir li*, God's beloved child. We want God's judgment to be clouded with *naches*, we count on the *kvelling* to trump the penalty we deserve, we want God's *rachmonus* to overwhelm God's wrath.

In the days ahead we will return again and again to the shaping power of the parent-child relationship. First, tomorrow morning, God will remember Sarah with the birth of Isaac. We will read of the lengths to which Sarah goes to protect him. We will read of Hagar's love for her son Ishmael. Tomorrow's Haftarah recounts Hannah's desperate plea for a child, and on the second day of Rosh Hashanah we will encounter Rachel's sorrow-filled tears on behalf of her children. The stories are linked together by a parent's love for their child. As for the tale of the binding of Isaac, it is the exception that proves the rule. The take-home message of Isaac's near-death experience is the uncomfortable realization that Abraham's love for God surpassed his love for his son. Disturbing as the story is (and it is), in the rabbinic mind, not only is there a reason for it but we leverage it to our benefit. Tomorrow morning (in the *zikhronot* section of the *musaf* service), we will ask of God to "Remember how [Abraham] bound his son Isaac on the altar, subduing his fatherly compassion so that he might do Your will with a perfect heart. So may Your compassion [God] overcome Your anger against us . . ." It is almost as if – it is exactly as if – we are asking God to reciprocate the extraordinary deed that Abraham performed so long ago. If Abraham, a man of flesh and blood, was able to suppress his paternal love in favor of you, God, can you not, as you once did for Adam and Eve in the

Garden, suppress your anger, see past our faults, act like a parent, and forgive us into the year ahead?

Because whether it is God's mercy towards humanity, that of our parents towards each of us, or each of us towards our own children, there is nothing more potent in this world than a parent's love for his or her child. It is not just that we would do anything for our children. The power of a parent-child relationship is that it is a relationship that you never give up on. Siblings will take their own paths in life, spouses sadly may go their separate ways, friends come and go. But a parent: A parent never gives up on a child. When that child does fail or sin or fall short, a parent never writes off a child's potential; in a parent's eyes, it is always the sin that is judged, never the sinner. The theology goes much deeper than "once a parent, always a parent." A parent always believes that their child's story is still yet to be written, a parent never loses faith in a child's capacity to turn things around. There is always, always, in a parent's eyes the promise of return.

Friends, our task over the next ten days is to grant to others what we ask from God. These Days of Awe are not just about relationships between parents and children – but about the myriad of relationships in our lives that are in desperate need of repair. Brothers and sisters, husbands and wives, friends and family – the real challenge of this season is not asking forgiveness, but granting it, propelled by the faith that others are capable of personal transformation. In identifying God's willingness to be compassionate, in identifying with our predecessors' ability to do so, we recognize that each one of us is capable of doing so, and not just towards our children, but towards all those seeking to return. Too many times in the past year, to too many people, we have closed ourselves off to the possibility that a person is capable of change. Not today, not in these days to come. In the words of Rabbi Yehoshua ben Perachia, now is the time to judge every person favorably. We must allow for the possibility of a person's inherent goodness, that his or her story has yet to be written, and whatever that person's failing may have been, now is not the time to give up on them. They may or may not prove worthy; that ultimately is not in our power to control. But today we commit that it will not be for lack of effort on our part that our most precious relationships stand in disrepair.

"Open for me," says God, "a gateway of repentance as big as the eye of a needle, and I will open for you gateways wide enough for horses and chariots to pass through." Like parent to child, time and again, God has proven willing to take us back. No matter our failings, we are still creatures worthy of God's love. This holiday we pray that our loved ones will take us back – that in all our shortcomings, we are worthy of being given another chance. So too this holiday season, may each one of us aspire to be godlike in our behavior, replacing our hearts of stone with tender hearts: hearts supple and resilient enough to forgive those who are seeking forgiveness, hearts capacious enough to make room for the imperfections built into our humanity from the very start.

The 615th Commandment

Twenty years ago this fall, my cousins Jonathan, Benji, Michael, and Rafi took a trip that would change their lives forever. As many of you know, my Manchester-born mother and Glasgow-born father arrived in America shortly before I was born. My mother's sister never left England. She married a boy from Leeds, and they went on to have seven children: six boys and a girl. Leeds lacked a Jewish day school, so being the *heimische* family that they are, they decided that their children, my first cousins, would make the two-hour commute each way, every day, to Manchester's King David High School.

That frosty fall morning was no different than any other day. The four boys, aged 16, 14, 13, and 11, put on their school uniforms, got on the train from Leeds, and switched over at Manchester's Piccadilly station in order to take the Overland Metro Link that would let them off just a short distance from their school.

When they got off the train that day to walk those final blocks, they knew that the seven men sitting on the railing were no ordinary hooligans. Not boys, not teenagers, but grown men began to follow them. My cousins picked up their pace hoping to create some distance from their pursuers. Wearing their King David school blazers, my cousins' Jewish identity was apparent to the eye and the anti-Semitic slurs began. The gang of thugs began to verbally taunt the oldest – Jonathan – while Benji, the second oldest, tried to defuse the situation, hoping to pacify them with gentle and no doubt self-deprecating humor. But the sharp words turned to thrown rocks, and before Jonathan knew what was happening, not only had he been kicked in the back, but he was head-butted full force, breaking his nose and rendering him unconscious. The thugs, however, did not let Jonathan fall to the ground. They had other plans; their viciousness had only just begun. One held his limp body up so the others could hit and kick him even more senseless than he already was.

Michael and Rafi, the little ones, ran frantically to the front doors of nearby homes pleading for help. The residents opened their doors and poked their heads out to see what was going on, only to shut the doors on the faces of my 13- and 11-year-old cousins. Benji stood frozen at the sight of his older brother being beaten. Surely, he believed, there would be a point when enough was enough, when the point had been made, the abuse would stop, and the bullies would move on to their next victim. Jonathan's body fell limp to the ground, unable even to curl into a fetal position as more rocks, bottles, and kicks were inflicted on him. It was at the moment when the ringleader of the gang shouted "Kill the Jew" that Benji's naiveté died. There would be no respite, no forthcoming humanity, no help on its way. He threw himself over his brother to absorb the blows – only to become badly beaten himself.

The details of what happened next are understandably fuzzy. My cousin recalls the boots of the gang members being replaced by those of security guards from the train station who finally arrived on the scene. Benji carried Jonathan the remaining blocks to the gate of the school, where the receptionist called for an ambulance. When my aunt, his mother, first saw Jonathan after he was taken home, she was in total shock at his mangled condition, his facial features beaten beyond recognition.

As for the gang members, some were eventually apprehended. The price they paid for their crime was an inconsequential fine of fifty pounds – to be paid in installments over two years. As for my cousins, their lives were changed forever. Since that day, Jonathan has suffered from debilitating headaches and general poor health. The year following the attack, he was afflicted with cirrhosis of the liver – necessitating, over the years, three liver transplants. Now a practicing attorney in Leeds, he has courageously built a life in spite of the on-going health challenges he has faced every day since the beating. My cousin Rafi, from that day onwards, was ever fearful of walking alone outside his house in the UK. My cousin Michael, now a promotional filmmaker in Brooklyn, developed alopecia soon after the attack, a condition of hair loss that has fortunately never interfered with his ability to be in the company of a good-looking woman. Benji, on the other hand, spent much of high school going to the gym, learning how to box and defend himself. Never again, he vowed, would he let himself be pushed around by anyone.

The responses varied from child to child, each one affected deeply yet differently – not only the siblings present that day but also the others who grew up in a household dominated by the shadow of the attack. When they went to college, my cousins were all exposed to virulent anti-Zionism and anti-Semitism on British campuses, a university culture that vilified and delegitimized Israel in ways unimaginable until recently in the States. For my cousins, for their family, that day was a pivot of self-understanding, learning who they were, and what it meant to be a Jew in Europe and in the world.

I share their story with you, however, not because I want you to know what happened in England twenty years ago, but because today, on Rosh Hashanah, on this day that we gather to check on the condition of the Jewish people and of our Jewish souls, I want to speak to you about what happened this summer in Israel and Europe and what is happening right now. While Jonathan's ongoing health challenges kept him in England, and Michael's career led him to America, Benji, Rafi, and the two youngest – Lauren and Alexander – soon enough made *aliyah* to Israel. Benji served on the front lines of the second Lebanon war and was called up again in 2012 for Operation Pillar of Defense (*Amud Anan*), where he was joined in the infantry by his brother Rafi. Alexander joined the armored corps serving as a tank driver and finished his term of service just this year. All three were called up this summer to serve in Operation Protective Edge. All three, thank God, are alive and well today, and all three enjoy the love and support of their parents, siblings, and extended family.

All of us, I am sure, followed the news from Israel this past summer, and those of us with Israeli family of fighting age checked in with them for updates as best we could. But between the sirens and the cease-fires, my thoughts inevitably turned to that day twenty years ago in provincial England. I wondered what it must have felt like for the brothers who shared that ill-fated journey from Piccadilly to now share a trip to the front lines to defend the State of Israel. I wondered if Rafi, uniform on and rifle in hand, called on to defend his nation, was remembering the day when he – a *yiddische* boy in his school blazer – banged in vain on a neighborhood door crying for help. Never again would he allow his safety and the safety of his brothers to be dependent on the kindness of strangers. And I wondered if Benji, now in his third tour of duty, was recalling that day when he froze in horror, believing that somehow his enemy would play by the same moral standards as he did. Never again would a naïve belief in the goodness of humanity lead him to hesitate in fulfilling his obligation to defend himself as his attackers prepared their assault. It would be his decision – his and his country's alone – to choose the moment and manner by which his destiny would be shaped and his safety secured. I wondered if, twenty years later, my cousins could see the accordion-like nature of their personal history playing out in the events of their lives. They remain the same cousins. When we see each other, as always, we share memories of our granny, and we joke about the common quirks of those two sisters who are our mothers. But there is no escaping that the underlying principles of their existence have fundamentally shifted – a transformation brought into full relief by the events of this summer. Only here, only now, only in Israel were they able to be safe – to be safe *because* they were Jewish, not in spite of being Jewish.

Lihiyot am ḥofshi b'artzeinu, "To be a free people in our land." These are the words of Israel's national anthem, *Hatikvah*. This is what the promise of the State of Israel boils down to: the Jewish right to self-determination. "To be," as Professor Ken Stein puts it, "the subject of our own sentence and not the object of someone else's." In 1762 Jean Jacques Rousseau wrote: "I shall never believe I have heard the arguments of the Jews until they have a free state. Only then will we know what they have to say." (Cited in Daniel Gordis, *Promise of Israel,* p. 116) The argument for Zionism is not that complicated: for a Jew to be free to express his or her identity without apology; to stand proud in the faith of one's forefathers and understand that claim not to be at odds with being a citizen of the world. To have a home of one's own, a place where the Jewish spirit is given national expression and extended its rightful place to shine in the community of nations. The promise of Israel is actually rather straightforward. What this summer demonstrated is our obligation to renew our commitment to her vigorous defense – because it is a promise that is under attack and needed today as much as ever. This summer has proven to us, beyond a shadow of a doubt, that no matter what the assurances of the Enlightenment and Emancipation may have been, time and again, again and again, Europe and the rest of the world remain inhospitable to the right of Jews to be the drivers of their own destiny.

Are we really so surprised at the vitriol and anti-Semitism unleashed this summer throughout Europe? Quite the contrary, I would argue, there is an uneasy feeling of déjà vu. Parisian Jews barricaded in their synagogues while cries of "Death to the Jews" are chanted. Jewish-owned businesses attacked with Molotov cocktails. In Germany, in Italy, in England, all over Europe, and for that matter, in South Africa, South America, Australia, and elsewhere, there were calls for violence against the Jews. A toxic mixture of neo-Nazism, radicalized Muslim Jew-hatred, and a liberal leftist strain of intellectual anti-Semitism that has rendered Europe a place hostile not just to Jews but to a whole series of Enlightenment values upon which modern Europe was supposedly established. When the French intellectual Alain Finkielkraut was asked by Natan Sharansky whether there was a future for the Jews in Europe, Finkielkraut responded by wondering whether there was a future for "Europe" in Europe, meaning, was Europe itself a place that could still house the nation-state values of identity, equality, and tolerance upon which she is based? When I visit my family in England, no longer do I walk the streets with a yarmulke on my head as I do in America. I can still feel the sting of fruit pelted at my face a handful of years ago as I stood at a London bus stop. I don't need a second warning. From street thugs to elected officials, from the resurrection of old prejudices cloaked in the politeness of pseudo-political garb to a resurgence of vile blood libel charges, and everything in between, the writing is on the wall. Not another Holocaust – God forbid! – that is not what I am suggesting.

Rather a sad and scary existence in which Jews are implicitly or explicitly forced to choose between loyalty to Europe or loyalty to Israel, or even worse, loyalty to being a Jew.

And while I risk stating the obvious, it is this very right to exist, this right to self-determination that the immediate enemies of Israel would seek to deny. Read the charter of Hamas, listen to the words coming out of much of the Arab world. Would it only be the case that our challenge was that of a few ill-intended and poorly educated Holocaust deniers. No longer are voices in the Muslim world denying the Holocaust; there are those calling for another one! There is no subtlety in the charter of Hamas: It states that every Muslim is called upon to kill every Jew everywhere in the world. This is not about moral equivalences, about who started the fight, about where a border should or shouldn't be, or about the terms of a hard-won compromise. As the peacenik Amos Oz recently reflected, when it comes to your very existence, even he, a man of compromise, has little place to go. In his words: "One cannot approach Hamas and say: 'Maybe we meet halfway and Israel only exists on Mondays, Wednesdays and Fridays.'" There is no moral equivalence between the Iron Dome designed to protect Israeli citizenry and Hamas-built tunnels created for the sole purpose of kidnapping and murdering Israeli citizens. There is no justification for the indiscriminate firing of rockets on Israeli civilian populations or the Hamas tactic of deploying human shields, a strategy, which, in the words of former President Bill Clinton, is "designed to force Israel to kill . . . civilians so that the rest of the world will condemn them."

The conflict between Israel and her enemies is not a simple one. Israel has an incredible amount of reflection, soul-searching and painful course correction to do to demonstrate she is indeed committed to a two-state solution. But when I think of my cousins this summer, I am filled not with thoughts of politics but with the emotion of pride. Pride that comes in the knowledge that I live in a time that a Jew in uniform can defend a Jewish state. Pride in the knowledge that Israel is showing the world that there is a Jewish way to wage war. Can you imagine any other country in the world, our own included, that, when acquiring a target in a civilian population, first drops leaflets warning of an impending attack, then calls every cell phone in the radius of the incoming threat, then sends a warning "roof-knocking" rocket, all in order to give civilians a chance to escape the targeted buildings? Can you imagine any other nation providing food, water, electricity, and medical care to the civilian populations of its enemies? Can you imagine Israel's enemies offering a cease-fire in deference to a religious holiday – as Israel did for her enemies? Israel has responded to those who would seek her destruction with an ethic infused by the Jewish values of self-restraint and the prizing of human life. On our solidarity mission to Israel this summer, I was astounded to hear of the great lengths to which the IDF goes to reduce the loss of life on the field of battle, often at the expense of the mission at hand and, on occasion, at the expense of the lives of its own soldiers. There is no such thing as a good war, but what I came to understand this summer was that at stake was not just Israel's ability to defend herself against an enemy, but Israel's ability to defend the ethos of what it means to be a sovereign Jewish nation. That a robust democracy can be maintained even when surrounded by enemies, and that even in the fog of war one must be vigilant not to lose sight of the Jewish values embedded at the core of the Zionist project itself – the values that are being defended in the first place.

Yes, sometimes Israel gets it right, and sometimes Israel gets it wrong. But here, too, we need to appreciate the broader brushstroke of history. Are we really meant to believe that a UN or European court of inquiry is positioned to sit impartially in judgment over the Jewish state? If the High Holidays teach us anything, it is that one's moral compass is evident not in the making of a mistake, but in the ability to be sufficiently self-aware and self-critical to acknowledge when a mistake has happened, own up to it, and correct it. Compare the swift and immediate arrest of the Jewish murderers of an Arab child with the self-congratulatory admission of guilt by Hamas for the murder of the three Israeli youths. Can you imagine Israel's enemies opening up a judicial process of inquiry regarding their military actions this summer as Israel is presently doing? Can you imagine Israel's enemies openly wrestling with the dissent of conscientious objectors as Israel has this past week? The promise of a sovereign State of Israel is that Israel must answer to its harshest critic of all: its citizenry. Our pride in Israel does not rise and fall based on any single error in Israel's judgment or any single ill-conceived policy. Not unlike our relationships with our own loved ones, we are both pained and gratified to see Israel struggle with the competing values and interests embedded in her soul. We here in the diaspora can gently and lovingly nudge Israel in one direction or another, but we know that at the end of the day, Israel's decisions must be owned by Israel and Israel alone. That is the blessing, and the burden, that comes with being a sovereign state: to make your own mistakes, to own up to them, and to change course when necessary.

As I think of my cousins heading to the front, more often than not, I pause in the knowledge that our mothers are sisters, an awareness that makes me realize that if not for the vagaries of family history, I could be them and they could be me. Aware of the comforts of my life, I am forced to ask what I am doing to protect the dream and reality of the Jewish state. As in the Hippocratic Oath, our first obligation is to do no harm. When I met this past summer with the leadership of the Presbyterian Church regarding their divestment decision, it was with deep consternation that I heard of the hundreds of Jewish activists present at the Church convention wearing black T-shirts bearing the slogan "Another Jew Supporting Divestment." You can imagine the tipping effect this had on the measure – it passed by just seven votes – influencing Presbyterian delegates who may never even have met a Jew before, never mind understand the full complexities of the Middle East.

The prophet Isaiah warned: *M'harsayikh u-maharivayikh mi-meikh yeitzei'u*, "Your destroyers and ravagers shall come from within you." (49:17) Israel does not lack for enemies, and Jews should not add to them. I am proud of serving as rabbi to a community committed to housing a wide range of views when it comes to securing a safe, Jewish and democratic Israel. But as in the quiet conversations we are having with our loved ones in the week ahead, there is a way to criticize that is constructive – that is filled with love – and a way that is not. American Jewry has a responsibility to leverage its political, social, and actual capital to stand shoulder-to-shoulder with our cousins in Israel. It should not be lost on any of us that the one piece of legislation our do-nothing Congress was able to pass before its summer recess was the allocation of $225 million in emergency aid for Iron Dome. To live in this day and age, with the unprecedented freedoms that American Jews enjoy, and not be engaged on behalf of Israel – on campus, on Capitol Hill, in youth education, or wherever your passions, politics, and pocket move you – is an abdication of Jewish identity no less egregious than any other sin of commission or omission we will list in the days to come. It was the late theologian Emil Fackenheim who, in the wake of the Shoah, called on world Jewry to fulfill a 614th commandment in addition to the 613 in the Torah: a commandment to survive as Jews so as not to give Hitler a posthumous victory. Survival is not enough. Today I give this congregation a 615th commandment: the Jewish moral imperative to stand by Israel each and every day of our lives.

Park Avenue Synagogue will always be at the forefront of support for Israel. As full-throated, unrepentant lovers of the Jewish state, we know the blessings and responsibilities that come with being born into *z'man ha-zeh*, this unprecedented time and circumstance. We will do what we are called upon to do: to travel, to learn, to advocate, and to support Israel. We will support those communities at risk around the world with our presence, with our pocket, and with our politics. We will lead the charge, and I call on you to join me in shaping that vision moving forward.

But when all is said and done, the truth of the matter is that there is something more Israel wants of you, something I know my cousins want of you, something I want of you. Because what they have told me, what any soldier will tell you, is that proud and committed as they are to defend the citizens of the State of Israel, they wish to God it could be otherwise. All my cousins wanted as children, all they want now as adults is to live freely and joyfully as Jews – *bli paḥad*, without fear, *bli miklatim*, without shelters. They want to find a nice Jewish mate, create a *heimische* Jewish home, get a good degree, a good job, and give back a bit to their Jewish community. In other words, what they want is no different than what we want – for ourselves, our children, and our grandchildren – to live freely and peacefully and productively and joyfully as Jews! The greatest contribution we can make to strengthen the bond between American Jewry and Israel is to make sure that as individuals and as a community, American Jewry – our side of the equation

– is strong. You can't ask someone to be more of a Zionist than they are a Jew. Without a strong American Judaism, there is no American Zionism. Without a strong American Judaism, there is no Israel advocacy. Without a strong American Judaism, there is no bond to be nurtured. What can you do to support Israel in the year to come? More than you know. But I would ask that your first step in this season of reflection be the most personal – and for many, the most elusive – to live freely and peacefully and productively and joyfully as Jews.

As we do every year at this time, as I am sure you do in your family, my cousins and I reach out to wish each other a *Shanah Tovah*. The other day I spoke to Benji, just back from his service. He is a heavy machine gunner, and he described to me how in the course of duty, he and his fellow soldiers position themselves against the enemy: each soldier looking up and down the line, holding their formation as they prepare to march forward, often under fire – at risk of death. When the call comes to hold the line, *yishur kav*, one's natural human instinct is to do anything but that. It would be far more sensible to keep one's head down, let the danger pass, and hope that help will come from another quarter. But neither he nor any one his brothers dared do that. They held their line, they took their stand, and then they moved forward as one, defending their lives and the lives of the citizens of Israel.

Friends, I know how hard this summer has been. The headlines, the pictures, the fact-finding committees, and the onslaught of world opinion; the defamation, the delegitimization – in the media, on campus, in the political sphere. Zionism isn't easy. It takes courage, it takes sophistication, and it takes stamina. You gotta want it bad. The easiest thing would be to keep our heads down and hope that someone else will pick up the fight so we can just move on with our lives without anyone noticing. We here know otherwise; we here will do otherwise; we here will hold the line. We will find our voices; we will educate our children and grandchildren; we will advocate, we will engage, we will support, and most of all, as proud Jews, we will love the State of Israel. The Guardian of Israel neither slumbers nor sleeps, nor shall we. *Lihiyot am ḥofshi b'artzeinu*, to be a free nation in our land – cousin-to-cousin, shoulder-to-shoulder, holding the line, fighting for a truly just cause: the preservation of the people and the State of Israel.

Yom Kippur
As a Driven Leaf

As a Driven Leaf stands as Rabbi Milton Steinberg's most famous book, and arguably, the single most significant contribution to the literary canon of American Jewish theology. Based on scattered Talmudic references, Steinberg's novel is set in second-century Palestine and tells the story of Rabbi Elisha Ben Abuyah. Elisha's mother died in childbirth, so he was brought up by his Hellenized father, until he too died, leaving Elisha to be raised by his religiously observant uncle. Blessed with a sharp intellect and probing mind, Elisha rises quickly in learning and stature to become a great sage of the Rabbinic Sanhedrin. Soon thereafter, however, Elisha's faith is shaken to the core as he bears witness to the death of the twin boys of his most beloved disciple, Rabbi Meir, and his wife Beruriah. The hammer to his faith, so to speak, would fall when Elisha beholds the death of a young boy obeying the command of his father to shoo away a mother bird in order to retrieve its eggs, fulfilling not one, but two biblical commandments associated with the reward of long life. At the sight of the pious boy tumbling to his death, Elisha's trust in God disintegrates: "It is all a lie," he said with a terrible quiet in his voice. "There is no reward. There is no Judge. There is no Judgment. For there is no God." Disillusioned with his faith and having uttered heresy aloud, Elisha flees from his community to Antioch in hopes of finding wisdom and truth in Greek culture. Despite throwing himself into Hellenistic philosophy, thought, and society, here too Elisha fails in his search for certainty. Bereft of God, bereft of community, Elisha is left a broken man tragically alienated from everyone and everything he once held dear.

As for so many others, perhaps as for many of you, Steinberg's novel was a turning point in my own religious journey when I first read it decades ago. In the figure of Elisha Ben Abuyah, Steinberg gave voice to much larger struggles between faith and reason, between Jewish and secular culture, tensions that are not just the stuff of historical fiction, but struggles present in all of our lives. Over the years, I have read the book many times and given away more copies than I can count, and I teach it whenever I get the chance. The insoluble dilemmas embedded in *As a Driven Leaf* remain as pressing today as they did in the time of the Talmud, as they did when Steinberg first drafted the novel.

But as I pulled the book off my shelf once again this past summer, I was prompted to ponder its significance in a new and altogether self-reflective way. You see, *As a Driven Leaf* was published in the seventh year of Steinberg's rabbinate at Park Avenue Synagogue – precisely the same juncture at which I find myself today. After arriving in New York by way of a Midwest pulpit, Milton and Edith Steinberg went on to serve the needs of a dynamic and ever-evolving Upper East Side Jewish community. I spent some time this summer poking around his archives housed in the Center for Jewish History downtown. He was, like me, engaged in teaching, preaching, fundraising, committee meetings, movement politics, Israel advocacy, and more – all the things we rabbis are called on to do. Most of all, he was – as all rabbis are – a pastoral figure, present at the lifecycle events of his flock, the "hatchings, matchings, and dispatchings" of the Jews he served. In other words, Steinberg was no ivory tower figure. He was, first and foremost, a communal pastor – a realization that prompted me to reconsider what his most famous book was actually about. "I put a lot of myself into the book," Steinberg would later reflect, meaning that this was a book that could have been written *only* by a congregational rabbi, a congregational rabbi at a moment in time and space analogous to my own. For Steinberg, Elisha Ben Abuyah's struggle to find God and to find a place in the community were not merely matters of esoteric contemplation. They were, I believe, a congregational rabbi's active thoughts in his seventh year on the two primary and interdependent vocations of every Jew in the pew: the search for God and the search for community.

Seven years in, permit me to offer two postulates about the Jewish condition. First, as Jews, each and every one of us is called on to stand in relation to two things: God and the community. Second, a Jew's relationship to the former impacts his or her relationship with the latter. Meaning, on a good day, when things are going well, we believe that God is good, that God is just, and that the world that God created is a good one. And when our belief in God is strong, our place in the community is also secure. The closer we feel to God, the closer we feel, or at least have the potential to feel, to the Jewish community. That said, however, the opposite holds true as well. When we encounter loss, when we experience heartache and grief, these are the days we find ourselves alienated not just from God, but from the community as well. How is it possible, we ask, as Elisha Ben Abuyah did, that a just God allows bad things to happen to good people? The divine presence eludes us, or even worse, betrays us, and so we take our leave of the community. I understand the thinking; it is actually rather straightforward in its logic: a causal relationship between our disbelief and our disaffection. In more theological terms, there is a correlation between our proximity to God and proximity to the Jewish people. The person who believes himself to be in exile from God stands in self-imposed exile from the Jewish community.

Just the other week, I received a note from a young member of Park Avenue Synagogue, sharing with me her reluctance to attend High Holiday services. She explained that her father died in 2001 and that she harbored such painful memories of sitting with him in synagogue in the months prior to his passing, crying together as they chanted the words "who shall live and who shall die." "I haven't been able," she wrote, "to come to Temple on [the holidays] because I get too upset hearing those words." A beautiful Jewish soul standing alienated at the periphery, locking herself out due to the theological assumptions of a synagogue. "There is no Judge and there is no judgment," her thinking goes, and thus, "there is no place for me in the Jewish community."

As a congregational rabbi, as your congregational rabbi, I am in possession of story after story of heartbreak and sorrow. For all of our shared joys, and there have been many, you have also invited me to be privy and present to the saddest moments of your lives. The loss of loved ones well before their time, parents burying children, horrific turns of fortunes, and betrayals of trust; men and women facing chronic and terminal physical and mental disease. I have recited *viddui*, the death bed prayer, with congregants and their families more times than I dare count, and we cry together at each other's side. We are no longer strangers; your pain is my pain, the heartbreak is altogether real. "Don't tell me," you have said to me on more than one occasion, "that there is order to the universe, that this is somehow part of God's plan." More than once, I have heard your silent or not-so-silent existential scream – how in the face of pain and suffering, a congregant has fled the theological perimeter of the Jewish community. How many times have I myself sought to understand the painfully elusive will of God only to find myself with more questions than answers?

I think what Steinberg came to acknowledge seven years in, what I acknowledge today, is that there are limits to theological reflection. Philosophize all you want, seek your source for some definitive, but there is something terribly humbling about serving as pastor to a congregation. An advanced degree in theology is of no use in a hospital room, a funeral chapel, or a shiva house. The child plunging to his death in the fulfillment of a commandment is not meant to be a literal occurrence, but rather a case study on the absence of God's justice in this world. Elisha's flight, Jonah-like, away from the community, represents the most natural human response to the most unnatural and painful circumstance. Steinberg was the greatest theological mind of his generation, but as a pastor to his flock, when it came to human suffering, he understood that all his erudition was for naught. Knowing the job as I do, I have to believe that on more than one occasion he was brought to his theological knees at the suffering of the humanity he served. Not he, not I, not anyone, has the answer to why bad things happen to good people. As Arthur Cohen explained in his biographical sketch of Steinberg, *As a Driven Leaf* was "an explanation of himself to himself, an articulation of why a Jew stays a Jew and why a Jew deserts Judaism." (*Anatomy of Faith*, p. 49) Steinberg knew the pain of his congregants firsthand, and from what I can reconstruct, his life was not without heartaches, losses, and sorrows of its own. Steinberg knew all the reasons not to believe in God, all the reasons why one would take leave from community. Nevertheless, the strength of his conviction, his faith in God and the people he served, impelled him to build a community whose driving purpose was to bring back those who would otherwise be lost to our people.

Which is why, I believe, the most critical scene of the entire novel comes at its very end, the scene that I believe must somehow reflect Rabbi Steinberg's response to the questions lodged in Elisha's soul – a personality who I now believe was literary proxy not for Steinberg, but for the Jews he served. Disillusioned and broken, Elisha chances upon his beloved student, the same Rabbi Meir who had lost his two young sons years before. The day, exactly like today, was not only Shabbat, but Yom Kippur as well. In riding a horse on this holiest of days, Elisha was in knowing breach of the Sabbath commandment; he had long since abandoned any concern for Jewish law. Nevertheless, Meir walks alongside Elisha, yearning for the company of his teacher to whom he had once been so close. The two men eventually arrive at the roadside marker signaling the communal boundary, the Sabbath limit, beyond which an observant Jew must not travel. "Here is the Sabbath limit," Elisha tells Meir. "You must not go farther. It is time for you to turn back." Eagerly seizing upon his former teacher's words, Meir responds to Elisha, "Master, you, too. Even as it is written, 'Turn back, turn back, ye wayward children.'"

Only this year did it finally dawn on me that the voice of Rabbi Meir calling on Elisha to return was the voice of Rabbi Steinberg calling his Jews back into the communal fold. "Turn back," Meir cried, even now, with all your doubts, you can return. Rabbi Meir made no claim to have the answers to Elisha's questions. If anything, having buried two of his own children, those questions weighed more heavily on his soul than they did on that of his teacher. But what Rabbi Meir knew was that although he lacked the answers, there was still comfort, solace, and support to be found in community. Both Meir and Elisha knew full well that throughout our lives there would be times of *hester panim*, when God's face is hidden from humanity and we experience an existential loneliness at the realization of God's absence in our lives. However, unlike Elisha, for Rabbi Meir (or, if you will, Rabbi Steinberg), the Jewish response to the vacuum wrought by God's absence is that it be filled with the overflowing presence of humanity. "Turn back, turn back," do not leave the boundaries of the community, bring your wounded self in from the outdoors. To paraphrase theologian Martin Buber: It is precisely at the moments when God's contraction, *tzimtzum*, from this world is felt most acutely, that we call on the manifold relations of humanity to gush forth. It is at the very moment that we feel most estranged from God, that as Jews we must cling most closely to the humanity around us.

Despite the strength of my faith in God, I readily concede the problem of pain. I don't know why bad things happen to good people, nor did Steinberg, nor does anyone. But as a congregational rabbi, I am not without arrows in my quiver; I have a response. It is the response to which I have dedicated my life, the response of human presence, the response of community. In one of her final interviews, the twentieth-century intellectual Hannah Arendt recalled the day when, as a precocious teenager of fourteen, she wanted to rebel, and so she stood up in the middle of her Hebrew School class and declared: "I don't believe in God!" To which the Rabbi teaching responded: "Well, who asked you?" (Hannah Arendt, *The Last Interview: And Other Conversations*, pp. 128-129) Ours is a tradition that not only allows religious questioning but understands the role of community as the vehicle for that questioning. It is not theology that matters as much as it is human presence. Technically speaking, according to Jewish law, when you show up at someone's shiva house, you are not supposed to speak until spoken to. You aren't there for your intellect, to explain someone's suffering to them; you are there to let another person know that they are not as alone as they would otherwise believe themselves to be.

I am reminded of one of Elie Wiesel's recollections from Auschwitz-Birkenau. One night, three learned prisoners, experts in Jewish law, convened a rabbinical court to put God on trial. Night after night witnesses were called up, some for the prosecution and others for the defense. Finally, after several nights of deliberation, the head of the tribunal announced the verdict for God: "Guilty as charged." Following a silence, lasting, in Wiesel's words, "a minute or an infinity," the head of the court shook himself, smiled sadly, and said, "And now, let us pray *ma'ariv* [the evening service]." The story reveals the paradoxical nature of Jewish faith – a sort of "in spite of it all" spiritual posture. We do not know the will of God, we may even object to it, and for that matter, nobody necessarily even asked us for our opinion. Yet, in spite of everything, we still turn to each other. In communion with each other we still pray to a God who is absent and perhaps even guilty as charged. Even at those moments, precisely at the moments when our faith wavers, there is always the voice of Rabbi Meir calling on us: "Turn back, turn back" to your people.

I cannot speak for all synagogues, only this one. And seven years older and hopefully wiser than when I came, I can tell you that our message today is one and the same as it was in the time of Rabbi Steinberg. "Turn back," we plead to you standing on the boundary of community. There is no theological litmus test for entry; we are not here to judge you. A synagogue is not just a place for believers; if it were, it wouldn't be so hard to get a seat. We will take you back. The promise of community is that it is a place that validates and honors your inquiries, provides you the space and tools to ask your questions aloud, and puts you in relation with other people of integrity facing the same or similar struggles. If you are angry with God, then this is a place to express that rage. If you are drowning in self-pity, then community will give you the strength to leverage your hurt towards empathy for the hurt of others. If God's presence eludes you, then it is in the presence of other human beings created, like you, in the image of God that will provide uplift. If you are without hope, then it is here, in the synagogue, that you will come to see that our world, though deeply flawed and filled with pain, is not without its blessings. If nothing else, this synagogue is a place that calls on us to express gratitude for the most basic gifts of our lives, gifts that we know would otherwise be eclipsed by the overwhelming pain in this world. Let this synagogue serve as refuge to you in this storm-tossed world. The gates of return are never closed; turn back, turn back to the Jewish community that wants you so.

In the heart of the campus of Tel Aviv University sits *Beit Hatefutsot*: The Museum of the Jewish People, and on display in one corner of the museum is a sculpture called "The Minyan," a scene of Jews, old and young gathering for prayer. The idea behind it came from Abba Kovner, the famed Lithuanian partisan turned Israeli poet. Though Kovner survived the Vilna Ghetto uprising, many of his family and comrades perished in the Shoah. Understandably, when

Kovner arrived in Israel, he was alienated from God, secular to the bone, wanting nothing to do with organized religion. One day, while he was walking through the Old City of Jerusalem, a man pulled on his sleeve and invited him to join a *minyan* at the Western Wall – to be the tenth. For the first time, Kovner explained, he felt he counted, that he belonged, that he was needed in the Jewish community. The oddity of the minyan sculpture, Kovner explains, is that it has only nine and not ten participants as prescribed by Jewish law. The absence of the tenth is meant to remind you, the viewer, that you are needed to complete the minyan, that the community cannot go on without your help. (Lawrence Epstein, *A Treasury of Jewish Anecdotes*, p. 128)

Friends, our world provides us with so many reasons to turn away. For far too many here, the year gone by has been filled with pain and sorrow. We know that so too, the year ahead will undoubtedly provide reasons enough to challenge our faith. I pray to God that neither you nor your family should know any suffering or loss. Please God it should be a good year for each and every one of you. But should it be the case that sorrow arrives at your doorstep, don't turn away; turn back. Turn back to the community. Your humanity matters. Without you this community is not complete, without you we cannot be whole. With all your doubts, with all your objections, and should it be the case, with all your disbelief, the integrity of our search is bolstered by your presence. Broken as your soul may be, it is in the presence of other such souls that we find the strength, together, to greet a new day. You and I, all of us together, creating a community capable of bringing the wandering Jew in from exile and maybe, just maybe, bringing a distant God, closer to earth, closer to each and every one of us.

The Revisitations of Yizkor

Over the next twenty-four hours, as we celebrate the festival of Simhat Torah, you might ask yourself the following question: Why do the Jewish people have not one, but two holidays to celebrate Torah? Tonight, of course, begins Simhat Torah, the "Joy of Torah." We conclude the reading of the book of Deuteronomy with the death of Moses and then, without pause, begin the story of creation in the book of Genesis. The Torah scrolls are removed from the ark, and with great joy and song, we, our children, and our grandchildren dance them through the community. And then there is the spring/summer holiday celebrating Torah: Shavuot, the Festival of Weeks, observed on the sixth day of the month of Sivan. Seven weeks after the Passover liberation, we arrive at Mount Sinai to receive the Torah from God. Two holidays; one Torah. No other aspect or object of Jewish life is granted this twice-celebrated status. Why do we need both Shavuot and Simhat Torah?

I think the answer, or at least part of the answer, may lie in the fact that while both holidays do indeed celebrate Torah, they reflect two altogether different aspects of our people's founding document. Shavuot is referred to as *z'man matan torateinu*, the time of the giving of the Torah. It was on Shavuot that Revelation, the giving itself, happened. According to some sources, Israel received the Torah with joy; according to others, under duress. Either way, Shavuot celebrates the relationship between God and the Jewish people, with the Torah as the object bestowed by the former to the latter: an enduring sign of our covenant with God.

Simhat Torah, on the other hand, celebrates a Jew's relationship not with God, but with the Torah itself. As we conclude one cycle and enter a new one, we embrace our status as People of the Book. *Parashah* after *parashah*, year after year, again and again, we read the same stories over and over. There are no surprises, we know that Isaac will be saved at the last minute, we know that Joseph will reconcile with his brothers, we know the sea will split at the critical moment. I am reminded of the story of two friends Abe and Sol who sit down in front of the TV to watch a cowboy movie, and at a certain point Abe turns to Sol and says, "I'll bet you ten dollars that the cowboy will fall off his horse." To which Sol replies, "You're on." And sure enough, the next scene comes and the cowboy falls off his horse. Sol reaches into his pocket to pay up, but Abe stops him, explaining that he can't possibly take the money; he admits to having seen the movie before. Sol responds, "That's OK, I saw the movie before, too." Abe asks, "Sol, if you saw the movie before, then why in the world would you bet me that he wouldn't fall off his horse?" Sol replies, "Well, to be honest, I didn't think he would be so dumb as to do it again."

To be a Jew means to be a member of the world's most obsessive-compulsive book club. We read the same story over and over; we know exactly how the story will turn out, and yet we read it again. Why? Because, as any lover of the text will tell you, every time we read it, the story takes on new meaning. The story may be the same, but we are, year-to-year, different people. Some years, we identify with one sibling in a rivalry; other years, another. Some years, God's deeds seem just; other years, cruel and unjustified. Simhat Torah teaches that it is not the story itself, but our relationship to the story, that makes us who we are. The message of Simhat Torah is not better or worse than that of Shavuot, just different. It is a reminder that it is the relationship we have to the narrative, and not just the narrative itself, that defines us as a people. And in this season's renewal of the scriptural cycle, we come to recognize a quiet truth about Torah's hold on us. The enduring sanctity of Torah is that, at one and the same time, it is both unchanging and ever-changing. Each one of us is empowered to find new meanings in a fixed text, an indeterminate number of interpretations, as numerous as there are readers of the Torah. Not the Torah itself, but the overflowing cup of its interpretive possibilities – that is what we celebrate over the next twenty-four hours on Simhat Torah.

Long before literary theorists knew about reader-response theory, Jews understood that the power of any narrative, Torah or any other, lies not in the origins or historicity of that story, but rather in our ability to draw meaning from that story and apply that meaning to our own lives. As Solomon Schechter famously noted: "It is not the mere revealed Bible that is of first importance to the Jew, but the Bible as it repeats itself in history." (*Studies in Judaism*, p. 15) At our Passover seders, we recall the Exodus not as an exercise in history, but as an effort to leverage that story of liberation to guide our own struggles. On Rosh Hashanah, we invoke the creation of the world not in order to establish chronology, but to remind ourselves of the creative possibilities embedded in our humanity. As the historian Yosef Yerushalmi wrote in his book *Zakhor*, while it may have been the Greeks who were the fathers of history, "the fathers of meaning in history were the Jews." (p. 8) No doubt, when we read, recall, and tell our stories, we do so with an eye to what did or didn't happen. But as much as – if not more than – the facts themselves, the Jewish act of remembrance, of Yizkor, is about making meaning; in other words, how we relate to the tale we tell, how we leverage that story into our own existence, and perhaps most importantly, the degree to which the story we recall does or doesn't impact the narratives of our own lives.

All of which, of course, is precisely the point of Yizkor, our service of remembrance. Fathers and mothers, husbands and wives, brothers and sisters, sons and daughters – we recall one or more loved ones, their stories all marked by a beginning and an end. The task of Yizkor is fundamentally different than the eulogies delivered upon their passing, the grief-filled words spoken at graveside. At risk of stating the obvious, Yizkor is as much about we the living as it is about the dead. It is here, in the Yizkor service, that we ask the question of how each one of us relates to the story of the lives of the loved ones whom we recall. Their Torah has concluded, but it continues to teach. We revisit their stories, as with the Torah, relating to them differently at every Yizkor service. Yizkor reminds us that the interpretive process continues. Each year our focus may change, a different aspect of our loved one emerges. With the passage of time, our perspective changes. We become different people and so our memories of our loved ones will inevitably change as well. Yizkor is not only an evolving experience, but it is meant to be empowering. In every Yizkor we are granted the opportunity to learn anew from the lives of our loved ones, their grace, their struggles and yes, even their shortcomings. Their humanity, no different than our own, was marked by imperfections. The task of Yizkor is not to judge, but to understand, to understand and to learn, and then of course, to apply what we have learned. The revisitations of our Yizkor prayers are meant to spur our own growth – continued efforts not just to honor the lives of our loved ones, but towards making our own lives worthy of remembrance.

The most moving scene of all of biblical literature is, I believe, the final passage of Deuteronomy: the verses relating the death of Moses. "Never again did there arise in Israel a prophet like Moses." (34:10) According to tradition, the final verses of his life were penned by Moses himself as his tears dropped onto the parchment below. Then a divine kiss took his soul, and it ascended to the heavens. We will read these verses, and then, seamlessly, direct our attention to the Garden of Eden, the creation of life. The same divine breath, *neshamah*, infused into Adam and Eve – death and life literally in the same divine breath: This is the message not only of the festival of Simhat Torah, but of Yizkor itself. To embrace those irreplaceable loved ones whose souls are now in God's eternal embrace. They have breathed their last breaths, and we today breathe deeply, seeking to fill our own lives with meaning and purpose guided by their memory. May their beautiful *neshamot* inform us, guide us, and inspire us, as we unroll the next chapters of the scrolls of our own lives.

Timshel

John Steinbeck may not be the most obvious place to begin a discussion on biblical philology and theology, but for the purposes of understanding the drama of the Garden of Eden, if not the human condition as a whole, it is as good a place as any. The passage can be found in chapter 24 of Steinbeck's famed 1952 novel *East of Eden*. Three central characters – Lee, Adam, and Samuel Hamilton – debate the meaning of the sixteen verses of the fourth chapter of Genesis, better known to us as the story of Cain and Abel.

Familiar as it may be, the background is important to review: Cain and Abel are the two sons born to the first couple, Adam and Eve. Both make offerings to the Lord. Abel's is received, but to Cain and his offering the Lord paid no heed. Cain is downcast and depressed, and God addresses him: "Why are you distressed and why is your face fallen? Surely if you do right, there is uplift. But if you do not do right sin crouches at your door; its urge is toward you, and you . . . *v'atah timshel bo*." (4:6-7)

Traditionally, the focus of our attention is on the subsequent murder of Abel, Cain's reprimand and punishment by God, and the consequences of the incident on the rest of human history. But for the characters in Steinbeck's novel, the focus is on that one word *timshel*, which I consciously did not translate. In the King James version, Lee explains, *timshel* is translated "You shall rule over it." In other words, God extends to Cain a promise that he will conquer sin. In the American Standard Bible, however, Lee continues, the word *timshel* is translated differently, as "Do thou rule over [it]." By this translation, God's words to Cain are not so much a promise, but an order: "Do thou," a commandment to Cain that he triumph over sin.

Steinbeck's Lee relates how, faced with competing translations, his Chinese relatives immersed themselves in the study of Hebrew in order to discover the true meaning of that one particular Hebrew word – *timshel* – a word that, in their estimation, was the key to unlocking not just the meaning of the biblical narrative, but "might be the most important word in the world." How that one word is understood, they reasoned, would clarify the degree to which, and the manner by which, a person can contend with sin and adversity. For years, the Chinese men engaged a learned rabbi, taking to the study of Hebrew grammar and vocabulary, eventually surpassing even their teacher's knowledge – all for the purpose of understanding this one word, which, after two years' time, they finally concluded meant neither "Thou shalt rule," nor "Do thou rule," but "Thou mayest rule." God's counsel to Cain was not that if he set his mind to it he would or should triumph over sin, but rather that he "may" triumph. In other words, it would be neither predestination nor obedience that would determine his fate, but his own choice. He "may" do it, but he also "may not." God had empowered Cain to make the decision on his own. Steinbeck explains that these sixteen verses are not just the tale of two biblical brothers, but "a history of humankind in any culture or race," a signal to Cain and all his descendants that "[one] can choose his course and fight it through and win." "Think," writes Steinbeck, "of the glory of the choice! That makes a man a man. A cat has no choice, a bee must make honey. There's no godliness there . . . But this [thou mayest]—this is a ladder to climb to the stars . . . It cuts the feet from under weakness and cowardliness and laziness . . . The way is open, the choice is thrown onto Cain and all of humanity."

As I opened up the book of Genesis once again this year, I was struck by the fact that almost none of the characters in this book, a book ostensibly all about new beginnings, is ever really extended the courtesy of a fresh start. Everyone is thrust into less than ideal circumstances. Think about it. Even before Adam and Eve arrive in this world, the tree bearing the forbidden fruit lurks temptingly in the center of the Garden. Noah is born into a world filled with violence. Over and over again, Abraham is tested. As for Abraham's son Isaac, having survived a near-death experience as a child, he spends the rest of his post-traumatic life triangulated between the love of his wife Rebecca and that of his sons Esau and Jacob. Jacob spends the first half of his life fleeing his past and his later years believing that his beloved son Joseph had been torn apart by wild beasts. As for Joseph, by the time he was seventeen years old, he had already been thrown into a pit and sold into slavery. Ishmael and Esau, Leah and Rachel, Dinah – any of them you name – the hand the Bible deals its central characters is almost always unfair. And nobody understood this painful reality more than Cain himself. As Elie Wiesel explains in his treatment of our narrative: "Cain . . . was guilty of no wrongdoing; he had transgressed no interdiction. Not yet. Indeed, he had not done or said anything as yet. Even his thoughts about God seem almost irreproachable . . . And what did Cain receive in exchange? A rejection . . . Offended, unjustly rejected, encumbered with offerings nobody wanted . . ." (*Messengers of God*, p. 45) Indefensible as Cain's act of violence may have been, there is no getting around that his story is a tale of a good person thrust into an unfair situation, placed into circumstances that were decidedly not of his own choosing.

And yet it is precisely this acknowledgement of just how unfair and unjust the circumstances are that Cain and his biblical contemporaries faced, that serves to clarify the nature of biblical morality. Steinbeck correctly understood that the stories of Genesis are driven not by the context in which the protagonists find themselves, but by the degree to which they wrestle with and triumph over the "thou mayests" of their lives. Abraham fails in his attempt to save Sodom and Gemorrah, but he is a hero because when he could have walked away, he instead chooses to argue the case before God. Jacob's moral rehabilitation occurs only when he puts himself at personal risk to reconcile with his brother Esau rather than deceive him as he did in the days of his youth. To the very end of his life, Joseph may have been a bit of a dandy and braggart, but history judges him a *tzaddik*, a righteous person, because when given the opportunity to lie with Mrs. Potiphar, he chooses otherwise, and, more importantly, when given the opportunity to exact vengeance on his brothers, he opts for reconciliation. Each and every biblical figure of note, at some point, stares a "thou mayest" in the eyes. They may choose one path, they may choose another; the calculus of biblical theology always insists on the choice being given. Our heroes are the ones who, when faced with the choice, choose godliness. Our biblical tragedies, as in the case of Cain, are those who choose poorly, allowing themselves to be overwhelmed by their baser instincts.

From the opening chapters of Genesis to Steinbeck to the narratives of our own lives, not a whole lot has changed. The stakes of our narratives may not be on a biblical scale, but I would dare say that each and every one of us has, at some point, felt the sting of being denied the courtesy of a proper "In the beginning." There is nobody who walks this earth, without, as my insurance carrier puts it, a pre-existing condition – physical, emotional, familial or otherwise. A challenge to our own health or to the health of a loved one, a loss, a setback that is not our doing but is, nonetheless, a circumstance with which we must contend. Not Adam and Eve, not anyone enters this world without a bit or a whole lot of adversity. Even if you are one of the lucky ones who walk this world uplifted by the blessings of your existence, even you too must know that sin always crouches at the door. We are all, always, just a half step away from sliding into the baser potentialities of human nature. Anger, callousness, pettiness, pride, brutishness, you name it, these behaviors may always be our fate if we allow it to be the case. The key word is "may," because they need not be. As American author Napoleon Hill once wrote: "Every adversity, every failure, every heartache carries with it the seed of an equal or greater benefit." Whether we choose to see that benefit, whether we choose to act to make that benefit a reality – that is a choice that is ours alone.

The title of one of Rabbi Steinberg's sermons, which became the title of one of his sermon collections, is "Only Human, The Eternal Alibi." Far too often, far too many of us see the limitations of our humanity as an alibi. Our behavior, our potential is self-circumscribed by our personal foibles and the cracks of this broken world that we inhabit. "Look at the hand I have been dealt, look at this world in which we live – what do you want from me?" We forget that as Jews, being aware of the shortcomings built into both our humanity and the world we inhabit does not permit us to avoid responsibility; nor for that matter, does it allow for our aspirations to be set any lower than they would be otherwise. To be human means to set the bar high. We are, as the prayer book teaches, a little less than angels – humans created in the likeness of God's image. We may always choose to climb that ladder to the stars. Each one of us is extended the choice whether to be a spiritual pauper or an aristocrat of the soul. Each one of us has the God-given potential for moral grandeur. In this new year, let us use the gift of choice wisely, and boldly choose to make the year ahead one of blessing for us all.

Noaḥ
Towers to the Heavens

It is not without some irony that 432 Park Avenue, the tallest residential building in Manhattan – and, for that matter, the entire western hemisphere – reached its peak just in time for the story of Tower of Babel. Towering over the Empire State Building, this 93-foot by 93-foot concrete megalith is reported to provide views from inside that surpass those of any other skyscraper and has forever changed the New York skyline. In my mind, however, it is not the view from within or without that is the most interesting view to consider, but given the coincidence of our Torah reading, the view from the heavens above. Looking at the building as I walked home every day this week, I wondered what the good Lord has been thinking these past months watching it rise up to the clouds. I wonder what God felt as it topped out at 1,400 feet. God must have thought, I thought, that this isn't the first time humans have built a tower into the heavens. I wonder if there is such thing as divine déjà vu.

This morning I want to take a look at the nine short verses that comprise one of the most enigmatic tales of the biblical tradition, the story of the Tower of Babel:

> All the earth spoke the same language . . . and they came upon a valley in the land of Shinar and settled there. One said to the other, "Come, let us build a city, and a tower with its top to the sky, to make a name for ourselves, lest we be scattered all over the world. The Lord looked down at the city and the tower which had been built and said "If, as one people with one language, this is how they have begun to act, then nothing they propose to do will be out of their reach. Come, let us

then, go down and confound their speech." Thus the Lord scattered them over the face of the earth; and they stopped building the city. That is why it was called Babel, because there the Lord confounded the speech of the whole earth, and from there the Lord scattered them over the face of the earth." (Genesis 11:1-9)

Despite the brevity of the tale, the curiosity and commentary it has elicited, as the tower itself must have, has been without limit. Never is it stated, nor is it ever clear, what exactly humanity did or said that prompted God's displeasure. Why exactly would or should God care if humanity leveraged its capabilities towards such a building project? Why wouldn't God take pride in a united and industrious humankind? Maybe the sin is not the tower itself, but as many have suggested, humanity's desire to make a name for itself? Or, as some biblical commentators have suggested, maybe the story is not about any sin whatsoever; maybe it is just a tale by which the ancients would explain the diversity of human language, in much the same way as the Garden of Eden story explains why snakes have no legs and women experience pain in childbirth. For some, the story serves as a polemic regarding urbanization, whether humanity should be concentrated or dispersed; for others the sky-high tower was the platform from which a rebellious humanity sought to storm the heavens. Or, maybe, like the Greek myth of Icarus, it is a story about hubris, of the dangers of flying too close to the sun. At its most basic level the story begins with a concentrated, unified people, a monolingual population, and ends with a dispersed, diverse, and multilingual humanity. To those who believe the tower to be the root cause of the problem, how curious it should be that at the end of the story the tower remains standing, just as it did at the beginning.

There is, of course, no single answer. Each interpretation contributes to our greater understanding. But as I stood the other day staring at 432 Park Avenue, it struck me that embedded in the tale is a lesson about humanity, our capacity for achievement, our boundless aspirational desires, and our need for limits on that very capacity and those desires. If the narrative pivots, as I believe it does, on God's realization that if humanity is left to their own devices, nothing that they propose to do will be out of their reach, then its take-home message lies somewhere in that realization as well. From Mesopotamia to Midtown, formidable physical structures prompt both awe and introspection – a reminder of our ability to reach for greatness and of the need to impose limits on that reach. Yes, the story is about the tower, but the edifice complex it speaks to is not merely about this tower or that one, but about the human condition itself. In other words, as we press against the envelope of our existence, as we marvel at the human capacity to leverage our individual and collective potential, is there a point when enough is enough, when more is actually less, when it is advisable, if not obligatory, to impose limits regarding what we seek to achieve?

If you read these first chapters of Genesis closely, you will sense a tension running through them, a tension at the core of every human being's spiritual disposition. Two somewhat contradictory sets of marching orders: the first reflecting humanity's ability to master, rule, and dictate the terms of its existence; the other reflecting a far more modest, humble, and restrained view of human ambition. For instance, in the second chapter of Genesis, we are told to till and tend the earth, to be stewards of God's creation; in the words of the National Park Service: "to take only memories and leave only footprints." In this formulation, humanity is subservient to creation, called on to protect and care for this world, but to leave it in as good, if not better, condition as we found it. On the other hand, in the very first chapter of Genesis, we are commanded to be fruitful and multiply, fill the earth and subdue it, rule over the fish in the sea, the birds in the sky, and every other living creature. Here, humanity is the pinnacle and purpose of creation, and we are called on to control, change, and impact the world in which we live. Which is it: the first or the second? Another example: on the one hand, we are created in God's image, just a little lower than the angels, called on to be like God in all our attributes. On the other hand, at the very moment we approach God's attributes, we are reprimanded, as we were banished from the Garden of Eden owing to God's fear that upon eating the fruit of the Garden we might become too Godlike. And following the flood itself came *both* laws establishing human mastery over the animal kingdom *and* a series of restrictions regarding the terms by which that mastery plays out. The list goes on, including, of course, this week's tale of the tower: Humankind's ability to build a tower reaching the heavens, and then the rejoinder that while it may indeed be in our grasp to do so, there are limits as to just how far we should reach.

If nothing else, these early stories of Genesis remind us that each and every one of us is a mortal, frail, and flawed human being. We look out at this world that we have been given, and it is only natural to seek greatness and attainment. Not only is it natural, but it is altogether admirable to want to leave a physical, spiritual, and intellectual footprint on this world. But there are also limits; though we may possess the spark of the divine, we are utterly mortal. We have our limitations: not every building needs to be tall; not every song must be sung; and not every sermon need be long. There are limits to what we can do and what we should do. As Ben Zoma taught: "Who is rich? The one who is content in his portion." As Abraham Joshua Heschel taught, the most important structure a Jew builds is not a physical one, but a palace in time - the Sabbath – our weekly reminder to cease from the human need to achieve and just be content with where we are and what we have. Some ladders are reserved only for the angels. Sometimes, the most courageous thing a person can do is to live within his or her means, within the envelope of his or her humanity, and inside the confines of our mortality. In this world of constant aspiration, conspicuous consumption, and elusive satisfaction, maybe this Shabbat can teach us to think not about what we don't have, but what we do have, to think about it, be satisfied with it, and most importantly, be grateful for the gifts of our precious lives.

Va-yera

Vive La France?

As I sat this past Monday morning in the pews of the Grande Synagogue on Rue de la Victoire in Paris, I could not help but be overwhelmed by a sense of history. It was the first stop of a non-stop three-day UJA-Federation Solidarity Mission to Paris. The synagogue was the site for our welcome by the Chief Rabbi of France, the rabbi and the president of the synagogue, and the president of the Consistoire, the representative organization of the French Jewish community. As is the case for many of you – as I spoke about on the holidays – of late my thoughts, concerns, and prayers have been directed towards our Jewish brothers and sisters in Europe. The most recent surge of French anti-Semitism includes the horrifying kidnap and murder of Ilan Halimi; the 2012 shooting in Toulouse's Otzar Hatorah Jewish Day School; the anti-Semitic, quenelle-filled "Day of Rage" demonstrations earlier this year; the murderous shootings at the Brussels Jewish Museum by a French-born terrorist; and the mob that besieged the Sarcelles synagogue on July 20 at the height of the Gaza conflict, among others. How could it be that the largest, proudest and most impactful European Jewish population now finds itself at the mercy of an anti-Semitic climate inhospitable not only to Jews, but to the very values of *liberté, égalité*, and *fraternité* upon which the French Republic was founded? With thanks to the leadership of UJA-Federation for planning a solidarity mission, I seized on the opportunity to go and get a firsthand sense of the situation and to return to our community not only to share my reflections but also to mobilize our community with a possible response.

It was not the beauty of the synagogue that overwhelmed me on Monday, but the knowledge that it was by way of that synagogue that Theodore Herzl arrived at the need for a State of Israel. The Synagogue de la Victoire was the synagogue of the French Jewish Captain Alfred Dreyfus. Dreyfus was married there just a few years before he would be arrested on trumped up charges of treason. Herzl, then a reporter for a Viennese newspaper, bore witness to the chants of "death to the Jews" incited by the anti-Semitic press and immediately understood the contempt in which Jews were held by their European hosts. Herzl's realization led him to formulate his own response to the "Jewish question," namely, a national Jewish home for the Jews: Israel. As Herzl reflected in his diary:

> . . .the thought grew stronger in me that I must do something for the Jews. For the first time I went to the synagogue in the Rue de la Victoire and once again found the services festive and moving. Many things reminded me of my youth and the Tabak Street Temple in Pest. I took a look at the Paris Jews and saw a family likeness in their faces . . . Was it then that I conceived the plan of writing on "The Situation of the Jews," or had I conceived it earlier? (*Diaries* Vol. 1, pp. 11-12)

As I listened to one community representative after another, I wondered – as did Herzl sitting in those same pews – if there was a future for European Jewry. I wondered if we are living through 1894 once again. The statistics speak for themselves: a ninety-one percent rise in documented anti-Semitic incidents in 2014 over the prior year; a three-fold rise in French *aliyah*, emigration to Israel. Excepting the blessed fact that Herzl's dream is now a reality, are we not living in an analogous moment? Was the purpose of our trip to show solidarity with a historic community, or were we, like the angels of our Torah reading, a delegation sent to warn our brethren to get out of their hostile environment before it is too late?

So what did I discover? After three days in Paris, what is the condition of French Jewry? As the old joke goes: In a word: "Good." In two words: "Not good."

First, the good. Not only is French Jewry not on the ropes, but I am happy to share that the French Jewish community I saw was robust, vital, and dynamic. Orthodox, Conservative, and Reform Jews, Ashkenazim and Sephardim, French Jewry is somewhere between five and six hundred thousand strong. Historic synagogues, state-of-the-art JCCs, oversubscribed Jewish day schools, museums that honor the memory of the Shoah, and Jewish summer camps, which – like their American counterparts – are the cornerstones for shaping the identity of Jewish youth. There is ample philanthropic and political capital. Over the course of the trip we met with the Jewish Vice Chairman of L'Oréal, Jean-Pierre Meyers; with the Jewish CEO of Publicis, Maurice Lévy; and with Eric de Rothschild, the Jewish chair of pretty much everything. Each one is a proud leader in the civic, business, and Jewish community. As for that classic brand of French anti-Semitism, though no doubt present behind closed doors, it is expressly forbidden in the public sphere. Strong anti-discrimination legislation means there are laws on the books to repress any racist, anti-Semitic, or xenophobic act. Remember, there is no First Amendment in France; even to contest the Shoah, or any crime against humanity for that matter, is a punishable offense. France has laws against anti-Semitic tweets, indirect discrimination, anti-Semitic comedians, all reflecting not just remnant guilt for Vichy France, but also the fierce protection of French values, notably the dignity of the human being. I was particularly moved upon meeting with senior officials at the Ministry of the Interior when one official shared that an attack on the Jewish community is an attack on the Republic itself. There is a close and cooperative spirit between the Jewish community and the arms of the government. There are neighborhoods in Paris akin to the Upper East Side to whom this entire discussion would seem odd – vibrant communities that are fully French and fully Jewish. As for the spike in *aliyah* numbers, relative to a half-million strong community, a jump from two to six thousand is not only not something to worry about, but could be something to celebrate – a lively Zionist engagement with the State of Israel. There is much good in the land of that gave us Rashi, Proust, and Ladurée – not just good, but very good.

That being said, I also saw much that was "not good"; in fact, much that I saw is downright distressing. Unlike Herzl, my concerns for French Jewry are not due to some congenital bourgeois brand of Catholic anti-Semitism. My concerns and fears stem from the emergence of a radicalized French Muslim community that, due to a perfect storm of events, has been extended a platform and wide berth to express a virulent and sometimes violent form of anti-Semitism against French Jewry.

As large as the Jewish community is, relative to the Muslim community – conservatively estimated at ten million – Jews are a drop in the bucket. Beginning with the Algerian war of the early 1960s, a North African population took root in France. But for a host of reasons, France has thus far failed to successfully integrate the immigrant community into the economic and social fabric of French life, a population that has grown exponentially since the 1985 Schengen Agreement and the creation of a borderless Europe. As you may well know, the standstill of the French economy has only made matters worse, with a general unemployment rate of ten percent and among the younger generation, upward of twenty percent. In a story as old as time, for lack of a solution or vision forward, it has been the Jewish community that has born the brunt of the attacks. Any religion, Judaism included, can be radicalized, and Islam has proven itself more susceptible than others. An ever-increasing number of disillusioned French young people travel to Iraq or Syria, are trained to hate and kill, and return to carry out the most ghastly attacks, which France, because of its liberal border policies, is ill-equipped to prevent. As for the mob violence, because it comes in the guise of legal anti-Israel protests, it is not subject to the aforementioned anti-racist legislation, despite the fact that the mobs are gathered outside synagogues and not embassies. You can only imagine how we felt sitting in the pews of the Sarcelles synagogue that just months before had been surrounded by hundreds of demonstrators crying out "Death to the Jews." Needless to say, the Muslim population has yet to express a scintilla of rage over the slaughter of hundreds of thousands of co-religionists in Syria, Iraq, or elsewhere. It is only lives lost at the hands of the "Israeli oppressor" that are cause for protest. The recent variety of French anti-Semitism did not begin with the Gaza conflict, but Gaza has served as a trigger and a useful cover for a much deeper hatred embedded in the radicalized Muslim community.

While it is the Jews of France who feel the most immediate sting of the changed demographic picture, the broader social and political landscape is adapting to the new reality in worrisome ways. Given the political force of the Muslim community, the radical left has understandably aligned itself to be in maximum sympathy with the Muslim community's grievances against Israel. As for the radical right, the Jewish community is warily watching the emergence of a mainstream anti-immigrant, anti-European Union, nationalist party under the National Front's Marine Le Pen. In other words, the current state of French politics has made strange bedfellows, which does not bode well for the Jews. As a representative from the Israeli embassy explained, French politics often takes the shape of a horseshoe in which the extreme right and the extreme left are closer to each other than they are to the center. And as for that vital center – because of the confiscatory taxation policies of the French government, France is experiencing an exodus of investment: first, of capital, but more importantly, a brain drain of young university-educated men and women, Jews included, who understandably are unable to see a bright future. Strong as it is, the French Jewish community is a politically lonely community, bereft of allies in an increasingly scary world.

So which is it? "Good" or "not good"? My answer, as you have heard, is "both." It is a decidedly mixed bag for French Jewry. But the more I thought about it on my flight home, the clearer it became that the Jewish community is only a bit-player in a much bigger drama playing out in Europe. Not only are Jews the scapegoats for the challenges faced by France, but we are the proverbial canary in the coal mine. Our present *tsuris* is only a precursor to the existential challenges on France's horizon, challenges ultimately faced not just by France, but by all of Europe. In the near term, I imagine the status quo for Jews will continue as it has, with periods of quiet, periods of unrest, and sadly, inevitably, sporadic acts of violence perpetrated against our Jewish cousins. In the long term, I believe that France, and by extension Europe as a whole, will have to address the more fundamental demographic clash brewing there. Much will be decided depending on how France handles its economy, its borders, and its politics. Thank God it is 2014, not 1894, or for that matter, 1938. There is an Israel, and if things were to get really bad, the French Jewish community could make *aliyah*. As Natan Sharansky reminded our group the other night, it was not all that long ago that twice as many Soviet Jews successfully emigrated to Israel, Jews who didn't have the resources of French Jewry. As American Jews, we can and must continue to support agencies like Masorti Olami (the European movement for Conservative Judaism) and the JDC, which work to ensure a vibrant European Jewish life. It is our support for the JDC and the Jewish Agency for Israel (JAFI) that, should the need arise, secures the safety of any Jew anywhere in the world. Most of all, it is our unflinching support of the State of Israel – even in, especially in, the face of withering world opinion – that provides ongoing reassurance to a nervous world Jewry.

My takeaway: French Jewry is fine, in some cases, better than fine. If it is ever not fine, God forbid, the existence of Israel assures that it will ultimately be just fine. As for France and Europe, I am less sure. Only time will tell – time, a whole lot of soul searching, and most importantly, a whole lot of hard work and bridge building to establish a Europe able to live up to the Enlightenment values upon which it was founded.

At the conclusion of our visit to the Sarcelles synagogue, the one that was attacked by a mob this past July, we were all so moved to be present that our entire group, to a person, were prepared to do just about anything to help, with trip participants literally raising their hands asking what they could give. And indeed the community leader did ask for something, something unexpected, something extraordinarily ordinary in nature. He asked our group of thirty-plus to walk through the neighborhood. Why, we asked? He explained that he wanted the surrounding community, Jews and non-Jews, friends and foes, to understand that the Jewish community of Sarcelles was not alone – that Jews around the world cared for them, stood in solidarity with them, and – should the need arise – would be there for them in their hour of need.

And so on that rainy cold day we took out our umbrellas and went for a walk through the working-class neighborhood of Sarcelles. It was the smallest gesture, one of healing, of *ḥizuk*, support, and maybe even muscle flexing for a community that I imagine felt so very alone just a few months ago. Big or small, ordinary or extraordinary, may all our gestures, all our words, all our deeds remind friend and foe alike that no Jew anywhere in the world ever stands alone. *Kol Yisrael arevim zeh ba-zeh*. All of the people of Israel are interconnected one to the other. *Am eḥad, lev eḥad* – one people, one heart, one destiny, in good times and in bad, now and forever.

Choosing the Right Pond

For those of you with two young children at your breakfast table, Cornell economist Robert H. Frank has just the experiment for you. For two successive days, perhaps as you would on any morning, take two glasses of equal size and fill them both with orange juice, each one to capacity, one for each sibling. On the third day, take the same two glasses and fill each one exactly half-way up. Finally, on the fourth day, fill one child's glass to the top and the other child's glass only three-quarters of the way. Now record what happened each day.

I have yet to try the experiment in my own home, but I suspect that the results I would get from my children, or you from yours, would be precisely the same as what Frank discovered to be the case. Neither child complains when both glasses are filled equally to capacity, or equally half-way to capacity. However, on that fourth day – when one sibling is given a glass three-quarters full and sees that the other sibling has been given a glass that is fully full – that is when the trouble begins: "The child with less looks first at his brother's glass, then at his own, then back at his brother's." Tension starts to build from within and then any number of actions follow. At minimum, Frank explains, there is an outcry to the authority figure: "He always gets more than me!" Alternatively, one sibling will try to switch glasses with his brother, who, though innocent in the entire matter, is seen as a hostile force. Does it matter that just twenty-four hours earlier a three-quarters full glass was entirely sufficient? In the eyes of the wronged child, of course not. Frank explains that satisfaction – or more broadly speaking, happiness – is not measured in absolute terms, but on a relative basis. The name of Frank's book is *Choosing the Right Pond: Human Behavior and the Quest for Status*, a title which tells it all. His guiding thesis is that as human beings our primary concern when it comes to status is not what we actually do or do not have, but about where we stand relative to others. Knowingly or unknowingly, we subdivide our reality into sub-groups or "ponds": familial, professional, geographic, or otherwise; and it is by way of those sub-groups that we measure whether we are happy, or as is often the case, not happy. As H.L Mencken once explained: "Wealth can be defined as any income that is at least one hundred dollars more a year than the income of one's wife's sister's husband." (*A Mencken Chrestomathy*) Human beings are funny creatures. We can be incredibly successful by certain measures, but be dissatisfied because we see what others have, and so we feel like small fish in a big pond. Or we could find ourselves in the most modest circumstances but feel on top of the world. Why? Because we see ourselves as big fish in a small pond. We see how much better we are faring than so many around us and that makes us feel, or potentially feel, very good.

Frank applies his thesis on the relative nature of status and happiness to large questions such as redistributive taxation, regulation, and government paternalism; given my one semester of macroeconomics, those topics are well beyond my pay grade. Nevertheless, anecdotally, his insights make intuitive sense. I recall my older brother coming out of his medical residency and being courted with two job offers. The pay was pretty much the same, but in one community he knew he could work less and live like an absolute king, while in Southern California he would have to work doubly hard just to make ends meet. I recall speaking to him about his internal debate and the respective trade-offs of the two options. Ultimately, rather than being rich, rested, and single in Tennessee, he chose to be overworked, underpaid, and married in California, and I believe far happier than had he chosen otherwise. Another example: my eighth-grade daughter is studying about Charles Darwin's famed passage through Tierra Del Fuego and how the ship's captain, Fitzroy, kidnapped three Fuegians, brought them back to London, immersed them in the big pond of English culture, Western clothing, and Christianity and was sure that once these now civilized Fuegians returned to their little pond home of Tierra del Fuego, they would spread their newfound, superior, "big pond" knowledge. The social experiment failed miserably. Once returned to their native habitat, the three "civilized" Fuegians promptly returned to their old way of life. In other words, unlike my brother who was happy being a smaller fish in the big pond of Los Angeles, the Fuegians were happier being bigger fish, so to speak, in a smaller pond. More simply stated, it is not always self-evident which pond people will decide to swim in. How it shakes out ultimately depends on the people and the variables of a given context. Nevertheless, if you want to be happy, at some point you have to decide. You have to know yourself and your circumstances well enough to know which pond you want, because once you are swimming in it, it is relative to others in that pond that you will derive your happiness (or lack of it). To do otherwise, to swim in one pond but always look to the other, to constantly measure yourself against a world that is not your own, that is the surest way to a life of dissatisfaction and heartache.

All of which, I believe, would have been really helpful advice to the first families of the biblical tradition. More than by parent-child relationships, more than by husbands and wives, the dramas of the book of Genesis are played out by way of sibling relationships and rivalries. We started with Cain and Abel, then Isaac and Ishmael, soon Rachel and Leah, and next month Joseph and his brothers. In each case, the stakes are far greater than a glass of juice at the breakfast table: the affection of parents, the love of a spouse, or the attention of God. After reading Frank's book, it strikes me that in each case the root of the strife can be situated in the relative nature of status and happiness. "His sacrifice is accepted by God, but mine is not." "He is the son of the favored wife, but I am not." "She is the one blessed with children, but I am barren." Each set of siblings is a case study for Frank's research. And no two siblings are more at odds, more filled with enmity than this morning's fraternal pair, Jacob and Esau. Yes, they were twins, but from the very first breath it was clear that these two would or should swim in different ponds. Their physical appearance was like night and day: Esau – rugged, red and outdoorsy; Jacob – a mild man who dwelt indoors. Jacob had the brains, Esau had the brawn. Esau had the birthright and the love of his father Isaac; Jacob had the love of his mother Rebecca and had the in-utero promise of greatness. Jacob and Esau are more than just people, they are archetypes; their story is a biblical phrasing of a philosophical or sociological question. Is it possible for two brothers, born of the same womb, but so clearly meant to swim in different ponds, to live full, satisfied lives of fulfillment and reciprocal love and affection?

We know, sadly, that the Bible's answer will be a resounding "no." The nineteenth-century German Rabbi Shimshon Raphael Hirsch explains that the failure of Esau and Jacob's relationship did not just belong to them, but also, and perhaps even more so, to their parents. In Hirsch's own words, "To try to bring up a Jacob and an Esau in the same college, make them have the same habits and hobbies, want to teach and educate them in the same way . . . is the surest way to court disaster. . ." Had Isaac and Rebecca appreciated the differences in Jacob and Esau's characters and temperaments, had they nurtured each son according to his respective strengths and directed them each towards his own pond, then, Hirsch explains, "with their own totally different natures [they] could still have remained twin-brothers in spirit and life." (Hirsch on Genesis 25:27) But this was not to be. In a passage no doubt reflective of what Hirsch saw in nineteenth-century family life, he marks out the road tragically not taken. There was the potential for Jacob and Esau to develop into their own selves, differentiate one from the other, celebrate each other's achievements, soothe each other in life's setbacks, and enjoy the richness of their respective circumstances. The potential was there, but it was never realized, and both Jacob and Esau lived with a feeling of perpetual dissatisfaction and resentment. What one brother had, the other perceived to be a slight; the blessing one received was understood to come at the other's expense. Neither brother could ever be absolutely happy, because each brother believed his happiness had to be relative to the other. In their minds it was a zero sum game in which the increased joy of one necessarily meant a diminution in joy by the other.

Not for another twenty-some years would Jacob and Esau finally be able to reconcile. Each one needed the passage of time to cool off, each one needed to develop his own family, his own livelihood, his own sense of self in order to realize that they could, if they so chose, embrace each other, celebrate each other, and each be happy with what he had. As we will read in the coming weeks, the biblical story of Jacob and Esau, thank God, ends well. They grow up, they learn to be comfortable in their own skin, and they learn to embrace each other. But in this week before Thanksgiving, a festival that forces us to consider for what we are thankful, we know it is a story that is not just about our predecessors, but about each of us and our own families. Far too often our own family dynamics are marred by the same ruptures as we read about this morning. All too often, neither we nor our siblings have figured out a way to sit together, literally or figuratively, thankful for the blessings of our own lives while rejoicing in the blessings of our loved ones. It wasn't easy for Jacob and Esau; it isn't easy for us. But we dare not wait decades as they did. Life is too short, and the relationships are too precious and too few. Before it is too late, we must learn to say to each other, as Esau would one day say to Jacob: "I have enough my brother, let what you have remain yours." It is easier to say than it is to do, it takes a conscious, active decision, but it is a task that is well within our reach if we commit to doing it. To be grateful for the blessings of our lives, to be grateful for the blessings of those we love, to choose our pond and to know the satisfaction of which our rabbis spoke: to be happy with our portion. *(Pirkei Avot 4:1)*

Parashat Mi-ketz/Shabbat Hanukkah
Where Do You Put Your Menorah?

Joseph never had to ask himself where to place his menorah in the palace of Pharaoh, but if he had, my hunch is that its location would have been as inconspicuous as possible.

Joseph's transformation from Hebrew prisoner to fully assimilated Egyptian was both quick and spectacularly successful. Having interpreted Pharaoh's dreams, Joseph is cleaned up, dressed in robes of fine linen, and has a gold chain draped around his neck. He is given Pharaoh's ring, a new Egyptian name, *Zaphenath-Paneach*, and a local wife, Osnat, the daughter of an Egyptian priest. The transformation is not merely physical - about externalities – but one of substance as well. When his first child is born, he names him Menashe, meaning "God has made me forget the hardship and my parental home." The second he names Ephraim, meaning "God has made me fertile in the land of my affliction." (Genesis 41:51-52) In other words, there is a correlation between Joseph's newfound physical and familial prosperity, his ability to adapt to Egyptian society, and his willingness to shed the vestiges and memories of his roots. What would take future Jewish communities generations to do, Joseph accomplishes in just a few short verses. So complete was Joseph's transformation, that he would soon stand face-to-face with his own brothers, speaking to them in his adopted Egyptian language, and they would have no idea that it was their own flesh and blood with whom they were speaking. Joseph's Jewish identity was so well hidden, one senses it may even have been hidden from himself. Even had Joseph's dreams anticipated the second-century Hasmonean victory, I suspect he would have kept his menorah – his symbol of Jewish pride – well out of sight.

The festival of Hanukkah is many things. A military victory of a few against many: how Judah Maccabee and his band of brothers defeated their Greek oppressors. It is about the cruse of oil found in the ruins of the Temple – miraculously lasting well beyond anyone's expectations. But students of the Hanukkah story also know that embedded within the tale is a story about assimilation, acculturation, and the ability of a Jew to differentiate against the dominating tide of a majority culture. As Rabbi Yitz Greenberg explains in his history of the festival, by the second century of the Common Era, Greek culture seemed irresistible. Like Joseph in his day, the elites of the Jewish community had shed their ties to Jewish distinctiveness, opting for the Hellenizing ways of their host culture. The Maccabees fought not just a military battle, but a spiritual one: a dogged spiritual resistance or insistence that despite every opportunity and incentive to do so, they would not "let the light go out" of their Jewish identity.

By this telling, where we do or don't place the menorah signals a lot more than a technical aesthetic choice; it serves as the historic telltale sign or bellwether of our Jewish identity. No other Jewish festival – only Hanukkah – legislates questions surrounding the visibility of its central ritual. Both in the Talmud and in the *Shulḥan Arukh*, the sixteenth-century code of Jewish law, we are instructed to display the menorah in a visible place, by a door or window, for Jews and non-Jews to see, thus fulfilling the mitzvah of *pirsumei nisah*, publicizing the miracle. That said, each text explains that in times of danger, when such public displays of Jewishness would be unsafe, one may – or even must – place the menorah inside the home, away from public view.

More recently, and more interestingly, in 1978 an intra-Jewish squabble took place between the then head of the Reform movement, Rabbi Joseph Glaser, and the then (and maybe still) head of Chabad, Rabbi Menachem Mendel Schneerson. It was at this time that Chabad began to erect huge menorahs in public spaces, most famously in Philadelphia in front of the Liberty Bell and in 1979 – in the midst of the Iran hostage crisis – in Lafayette Park near the White House. Though the debate between Glaser and Schneerson was ostensibly about the constitutional issues surrounding the display of religious symbols on government property, at stake was a far more subtle and substantive question. For Rabbi Glaser of the Reform movement, Chabad's huge menorahs were a sort of aggressive exhibitionism – a public display of Jewish pride taken one step too far. For the Lubavitcher Rebbe on the other hand, these public menorahs were part-and-parcel of the mission of Chabad. Like the ancient Hellenists, he said, "many of our brethren have left us and accepted idolatry as a way of life." "We must be like that faithful band of Hasmoneans, [and] remember that there is always a drop of . . . pure olive oil" hidden deep in the heart of every Jew, which, if kindled, "bursts into big flames." (Quoted in D. Ashton, *Hanukkah in America*, pp. 243-245) The debate was not just about tactics, whether outreach should or should not take place in public space. At the core of the debate was how these great rabbis understood their comfort and discomfort in the American context. Should Judaism be public or private; do we live in a time of danger or comfort? As goes the menorah, so, too, Jewish identity.

We are living neither in the sixteenth century, nor for that matter, the twentieth century, but in a new era in American Jewish life. So let me put the question directly to you: Where is your menorah? At kiddush you can tell me the precise location in your home, but for the moment my question to you is more metaphysical than physical. Not just about how you feel, about whether being Jewish is core to who you are. Rather, does the light of your Jewish identity shine forth in your day-to-day existence, or is it something you keep hidden out of sight? At home, at work, on the street, or at play, does the fact that you are Jewish differentiate you from those around you? Simply put, do you live proudly and distinctly as a Jew?

The question is a simple one, but no doubt it makes us squirm. "What do you mean, Rabbi? Of course I live proudly as a Jew, my 'menorah,' if you will, is there for all to see." For some of you, that may be true. But let me probe a little deeper. Were you to do a self-inventory of the week gone by (Hanukkah candles aside), did you live a distinctly Jewish life? Observing Jewish law is the most obvious measure: Was there anything you did or – more interestingly – did not do, eat, or say because of Jewish law? What about your words? Do the people around you know you to be a vocal supporter of Israel, or do you shy away from those conversations for fear of taking a stand on a controversial subject? What about your home? Beyond the *mezuzah* on the door, would someone walking into your home know by the art, the books, the rhythms of your home, that yours is a Jewish one? What about how you spend your time and money? If I had an Excel spreadsheet of the volunteer hours and charitable dollars you have spent this year, would I be able to distinguish – or more importantly – would *you* be able to distinguish your allocations from those of a non-Jewish New Yorker?

Unlike those other moments in Jewish history, I think the question of menorah placement is different for us. Thank God, we are not living in a time of danger. Arguably never before in all of Jewish history has a diaspora Jewish community had it as good as we do here in America. But in all that comfort, we have lost our ability to articulate our distinctive Jewish presence and voice. Fun as it may be to point out Jewish Nobel prize winners, the "who's a Jew?" game doth not ensure Jewish continuity. Ours is an America, depending on your generation, of Stretch Cunningham from *Archie Bunker*, Ross from *Friends*, or Baby from *Dirty Dancing* – Jews whose Jewishness is understood but not spoken. We smile or cringe at the knowledge that Jerry Seinfeld, Sarah Silverman, and Jon Stewart are Jewish, but it is not at all evident to me that their work moves the needle of Jewish continuity in a positive direction. In all the news of this past week, you may have missed that Leon Wieseltier and Franklin Foer resigned from their positions at *The New Republic*, a sign understood by many as the crumbling of the tradition of the American Jewish public intellectual, the idea that there is a differentiated and critical contribution Jews make – as Jews – to American discourse.

Journalism, entertainment, politics – by any measure, the distinctive place of Jewish life in America is on the wane. Not the oppression of tyrants, and not even the allure of foreign culture is at the root of the modern-day Hanukkah dilemma. Our problem is rather that despite the freedom to do so, somewhere along the way we have lost our ability to articulate a passionate argument for Jewish distinctiveness. The promise of America is not a melting pot, in which differences between faiths are elided into one indistinguishable stew. The promise of America, to appropriate Horace Kallen's imagery, is that of an orchestra of different instruments in which each one makes a unique contribution to the symphony of American life. Merely living in New York surrounded by other Jews fails the test of our Maccabee predecessors. We can participate fully in Jewish life – but we don't. We can send our kids to Jewish summer camps – but we choose otherwise. We can set a communal value that Jews aspire to marry other Jews – but I fear far too many are fumbling this basic talking point. Different does not mean better or worse. Different means that the Jewish people have a role to play here in this world, without which our collective humanity would be diminished. It is not just humanity that needs the Jews, but the Jewish people that needs you. In this festival of lights, ask yourself, press yourself, about the degree to which you do or do not contribute to the light of Jewish life in all its manifestations – ritual, communal, cultural, intellectual, philanthropic, and beyond. This is the litmus test of our Hanukkah lights.

Eventually, we know, Joseph will reveal his true identity, reconcile with his brothers, and be reunited with his father Jacob in Egypt. The final scene of Jacob's life will have Joseph bringing his children, Jacob's grandchildren, near for a final blessing from the great patriarch of our people. In what are perhaps two of the most heartbreaking words of the Bible, Jacob motions to the boys and asks Joseph "*Mi eleh*, who are they?" Jacob does not recognize his grandchildren. The commentators explain that he could not differentiate his own flesh and blood from typical Egyptian youths.

Joseph was many things worthy of emulation, but a model for the transmission of Jewish identity was not one of them. Successful as he was, he failed to give his own children a sense of what being Jewish meant in the diaspora, and by the time he got around to it, it was too late. It is a gulp moment of the highest order to realize that the blessing and challenge of being Jewish in America is that if we fail to live differentiated Jewish lives, we have nobody to blame but ourselves. The decision of where you put your menorah is yours and yours alone. On this Shabbat of Hanukkah may we commit to living and displaying it proudly and prominently.

Sh'mot

In Memory of Rabbi Harold Schulweis, z"l

"I Will Be What I Will Be"

It is, and will forever be, a humbling proposition to serve as a congregational rabbi in the wake of the life and legacy of Rabbi Harold Schulweis, of blessed memory. Rabbi Schulweis, the senior rabbi of Valley Beth Shalom in Southern California, passed away last month at age 89. I cannot claim to have had a close relationship with him. I recall many Shabbat mornings in the hallways of his synagogue when I was a child on the bar mitzvah circuit, and when I was a rabbinical student at the University of Judaism, my classmates and I were always captivated by his occasional public lectures. If you have never heard of Rabbi Schulweis, his stature is best summed up in a tribute given by Rabbi Uri Herscher, who reflected: "Harold Schulweis is a rabbi. This is a little like saying, a Rembrandt is a painting. Or a Stradivarius is a violin. Harold Schulweis is more than a rabbi. He is a rabbi of rabbis. He is a teacher, a writer, a poet of the pulpit, a prophet of justice, a thinker of astounding power and insight. Truly, to read Harold Schulweis, to hear Harold Schulweis, is a transformative experience. He has, as much as any rabbi of our time, given Judaism meaning, relevance, and renewed purpose." (Schulweis Eulogy, December 21, 2014)

There was a prophetic element to Schulweis's career as a congregational rabbi. Much of what we take for granted in synagogue life was actually pioneered by him. Long before the PAS "Shabbat Supper Club," Schulweis introduced Chavurot into his congregation – "small groups of families to share religious life and family celebrations." It was Schulweis who long ago innovated with a "para-rabbinic" initiative whereby synagogue members were empowered and trained to support each other in times of need – the model for our own *Mercaz Hesed*/Caring Network and similar initiatives of so many other congregations. Decades ago, Schulweis was already pioneering inclusion efforts to welcome children with differentiated needs and their families – an effort that we are crafting in earnest at Park Avenue Synagogue today. Long before our own efforts to reach out to would-be Jews-by-Choice, Schulweis was leading the charge. Nearly two decades before the leadership at PAS announced its decision to embrace and officiate at the wedding ceremonies of same-sex couples, Rabbi Schulweis was one of the first Conservative rabbis to openly welcome gay and lesbian Jews into the synagogue. If, as the expression goes, imitation is the sincerest form of flattery, then it is not an understatement to say that a good deal of North American congregational life, our own included, is a collective homage to the vision of this one rabbi.

Were it the case that Rabbi Schulweis did all these things, leading the largest Conservative congregation in the Western United States for 45 years, we could – as the song goes – say *dayenu*, it would be enough. But as his obituary recounts, he did so much more. In the 1960s, having heard the story of a Jew rescued from the Nazis by a German Christian, Schulweis founded what would become the Jewish Foundation for the Righteous – recognizing, celebrating, and supporting thousands of Christians who rescued Jews during the Holocaust. Many of us were in attendance last month at the packed Waldorf Astoria ballroom at JFR's annual dinner, hosted by Harold's cousin, our own Harvey Schulweis. Or what about MAZON, the Jewish Response to Hunger, an organization that asks families to dedicate three percent of the cost of weddings or bnei mitzvah celebrations to feed the hungry? That, too, was Schulweis's idea. Some of you, I am sure, support the sacred work of Jewish World Watch, the largest grassroots anti-genocide organization in the world. Again, an initiative of Schulweis, who sought to make the Jewish post-Holocaust *cri de coeur* "Never Again" into a programmatic demand that the Jewish community never stand idly by in the face of contemporary genocides in Darfur, Congo, and elsewhere. (T. Tugend, Schulweis Obituary, *Jewish Journal of Los Angeles*)

As a *gadol ha-dor*, a giant of his generation, Rabbi Schulweis will undoubtedly be the subject of articles, books and dissertations in the future. It would be presumptuous, on the verge of unseemly, to try to distill such a storied career as his into a single sermon. Rather, in light of his passing, this morning I would like to focus on one aspect of this morning's Torah reading that I believe provides a critical key to unlocking his theological and professional vision.

The scene is perhaps one of the most familiar of our entire tradition: Moses at the burning bush. God has heard the cry of the suffering Israelites and calls on Moses to go before Pharaoh to demand their freedom. Worried as much about addressing his Israelite brethren as about his anticipated showdown with Pharoah, Moses inquires of God: "When I come before the Israelites announcing that I have been sent to liberate them, who exactly should I tell them sent me?" More than anything, Moses is desperate to get God's name, a concrete title by which God can be known. Famously, however, God deflects or rejects Moses' inquiry, responding *Ehyeh-a sher-ehyeh*, "I will be what I will be." Thus shall you say to the Israelites: "*Ehyeh*, 'I Will Be,' sent me to you."

It is, without a doubt, an enigmatic exchange. For Schulweis it is also a critical window into the nature of God. It was understandable that Moses wanted a name, a noun, a label by which God's being could be concretized. But as Schulweis explains in his treatment of this verse, "God is not a static noun, but a dynamic verb encompassing past, present, and future states of being." *Ehyeh asher ehyeh* /I will be what I will be. "God," writes Schulweis, "is not a subject or an object. God is known only in relationship and only in situations that bear upon man." (*For Those Who Can't Believe*, p. 136)

Schulweis advocated for what he called "predicate theology." If God was going to reveal the truth about the divine nature, it was going to be to Moses at the burning bush. Schulweis proposed an alternative way to think about God, shifting the focus "from noun to verb, from subject to predicate, from God as person to Godliness." (p. 133) It is only natural for us as human beings, as it was for Moses, to want to assign an identity to God, to think of God as a person or a noun. But while that is understandable, Schulweis explains, essential to our belief is "not the qualities of divinity, but the divinity of the qualities." (p. 133) "I will be what I will be." It is impossible to know God, but we can know Godly behavior. When we bless God for feeding the hungry, clothing the naked, or healing the sick, we are actually drawing attention to the human capacity for the "divine activities," the gerunds of "feeding," "clothing," or "healing." Neither we, nor even Moses, ever fully knows God, but we can come to realize the divine in human activity by way of how we relate to each other and this world. It is a theology that empowers humanity to seek to make real God's will on this earth. "I will be what I will be." Don't worry so much about my name, about the nouns, God says, worry about the verbs, about making my attributes alive in this universe. Compassion, ethics, kindness, integrity, generosity – anything that elevates the humanity of another, that helps another arrive at his or her God-given potential – that is Godly behavior.

Schulweis's predicate theology is not without its flaws, but it is a theology that resonates strongly in our day and age. Tellingly, the book in which Schulweis articulates his theological position is called *For Those Who Can't Believe*. Schulweis provides a template by which every human being, even those who struggle with faith, can engage in religious language and behavior. Where is God in sickness or in a tsunami? Our world provides ample reason for disbelief. Predicate theology may not have all the answers, but it provides the opportunity and obligation for each of us to respond to such crisis moments with activities that restore God's presence to this world. It is a theology that depends on human activity in that the choices we make ultimately determine the degree to which humanity experiences the divine. God is not a proposition that can be proved or disproved. God, rather, is the "good that we do" – should we choose to do it.

Which is why, I believe, there is a direct connection between Schulweis's theology and his extraordinary rabbinic career. To build a community that supports each other in times of need, that treats every human being – straight, gay, Jew, non-Jew – as equal in the eyes of God, this is to create a community filled with God's presence. To devote one's energies to feeding the hungry, stopping genocide, honoring the righteous gentiles of the Shoah, these are efforts that collectively give expression to God's will. I do hope people find God when they come to a synagogue to pray, but statistically speaking, that will not be the case for every one of us, every time. So how thrilling is it to think of a synagogue as an institutional opportunity to actualize God's presence on earth? Schulweis's congregational legacy is not just worthy of detached study but of enthusiastic emulation. We can and should be responsive to the issues of the day. We can and should mobilize to repair the fractures in this broken world. As human beings created in the image of God, as a synagogue charged to house God's presence, we can and should understand ourselves as agents in making God's attributes felt in this world.

Most of all, Schulweis's predicate theology is a reminder that each one of us, created in God's image, is a dynamic being who will "be what we will be." The Exodus story, at its core, is a tale of becoming. Moses who transcends his station and self-perceived limitations to lead a nation. The children of Israel who learn to see beyond the horizon of their enslavement and into the Promised Land. It should not be missed that the antagonist of this tale is Pharaoh – whose static disposition, whose hardened heart, proves to be his undoing. "I will be what I will be." There is something God-like about seeing yourself as capable of ongoing personal transformation, of being in a constant state of becoming. Don't try to label me, for my today need not be my tomorrow. Growth, renewal – these are divine qualities embedded in each one of us. Whether we choose to access them or not – that is nobody's decision but our own.

At Schulweis's funeral service, my teacher and colleague, now senior rabbi of Valley Beth Shalom, Rabbi Eddie Feinstein sought to sum up Schulweis's philosophy with one of Schulweis's favorite parables. "When the angels heard that God intended to create man in his own image, they became jealous and plotted how to hide the divine image. One suggested hiding the image in the deepest ocean, another on top of the highest mountain, but the other angels objected that man would find it nevertheless. Finally, the wisest angel came up with a solution, saying: 'Plant the divine image in man's heart, and he will never find it.'" That, Feinstein concluded, "was the essence of what Rabbi Schulweis taught us . . . God is not above us but in our own acts and words

. . . Divinity is within us." (Schulweis Eulogy, December 21, 2014)

Planted deep in our souls sits the potential to bring God into our world. We can choose, we can act, we can transform the world. Created in the image of God, we have the divine spark within, ready to be leveraged. We need to make the effort to find it, nurture it, and render it evident in all that we do. As individuals and as a congregation, may we endeavor to do so, thus not only honoring the memory of a great leader of our people, not only prompting us to live lives of constant renewal, but also committing to transform the world to be what we will make it to be – filling it with the presence of God's glory.

Va-era

Rules for Rabbis

On the 541st and, for that matter, final page of Sanford Horwitt's biography of Saul Alinsky, Horwitt reveals the story that he believes is the defining moment in the life of one of our nation's most provocative and impactful community organizers. Born to Russian Jewish parents in Chicago in 1909, Saul David Alinsky led many of our country's most significant movements for social change over the course of his lifetime. From addressing societal ills in Chicago's South Side neighborhoods to the civil rights movement, from the antiwar movement of the 1960s to mentoring Cesar Chavez's United Farm Workers, Alinsky was in many respects the founding father of modern community organizing. From his founding of the Industrial Areas Foundation (IAF) to his famous book on community organizing, *Rules for Radicals*, Alinsky's institutional and intellectual legacy extends well beyond his untimely death in 1971, shaping generations of community organizers, not the least of whom is President Obama.

Horwitt shares that when Alinsky "was twelve years old and living on the old West Side [of Chicago], one day a friend of his was jumped and beaten by three kids from the nearby Polish neighborhood of West Crawford Avenue. 'So naturally, [continued Alinsky] we went on the hunt and found a couple of Poles.' Alinsky remembered, 'We were merrily beating them up when the police suddenly appeared and arrested all of us.'" The boys were taken to the police station, where their mothers soon appeared, screaming that the boys had disgraced their families and would be punished when they got home.

But Alinsky's mother first took her son to their rabbi, and the rabbi lectured him about how wrong he was. Young Sollie defended himself:

> "They beat up my friend," I said. "So we beat them up. That's the American way. It's also in the Old Testament: 'an eye for an eye, a tooth for a tooth.' Beat the hell out of them. That's what everybody does."
>
> The rabbi answered, "You think you're a man because you do what everybody does. Now I want to tell you something that the great Rabbi Hillel said: 'Where there are no men, be thou a man.' I want you to remember that."
>
> "I've never forgotten it," Alinsky said, a lifetime later. (Horwitt, *Let Them Call Me Rebel*, p. 541)

B'makom she-ein anashim, hishtadel lihiyot ish, "In a place where there are no men, be thou a man." *[Pirkei Avot 2:6]* If nothing else, this weekend's commemoration of Martin Luther King's legacy reminds us of the ability of a single person to organize a social movement and bring about change: To see the ills, inequalities, and abuses of an unjust society, and choose not to do what everyone else does, neither to be frozen into inertia nor prompted to violence, but to organize and mobilize towards redressing and fixing the fractures of our broken world.

Given the confluence of the weekend's commemoration and the Torah reading's dramatic tale of liberation, I want to focus not so much on any one particular social issue, but to draw on the Exodus narrative as a manual for community organizing – to interweave the writing of Alinsky and the Almighty, and offer my own "Rules for Rabbis." In other words, what lessons can we learn about community organizing from the most famous community organizer of all: Moses himself.

Let's begin with the qualifications of Moses to be a community organizer. At first blush, the most interesting thing to say about Moses' leadership qualities is that he seems to have none. It is not his pedigree – he comes from nowhere; it is not his speaking ability, which we know to be deficient; it is not his confidence, which we know to be lacking; it is not in his spine of steel – he kvetches until his final day. It is certainly not his ability to keep cool under fire. From killing the Egyptian to the Golden Calf to striking the rock, Moses demonstrates a repeated proclivity to fly off the handle. So what was Moses' distinctive leadership quality? In a word: empathy. From the very beginning to the very end, Moses was predisposed to see someone else's problems and make them his own. Having grown up in Pharaoh's house, Moses "goes out to see his brethren." More than signaling physical movement, this verse denotes empathy; he sees their burdens, he sees that there is no one taking action, and, as Rabbi Hillel teaches and Alinsky learned, he rises to the occasion. What is rule number one of organizing? Empathy.

Next is the story of the burning bush, where God reveals the divine self and speaks to Moses in a way no other human has experienced since. It is a mystical encounter, but on a more basic level, it is a relational meeting, an introductory coffee, or in organizing-speak, a "one-on-one." As any community organizer will tell you, the secret to any social movement is relationship building. You find out what makes someone tick, you explore that person's values, find out what is important to him or her. You build a connection, which becomes a trust, which in turn, becomes social capital. You learn the stories, commitments, and passions that make someone act, and in that dialogue you build common cause. Communities do not emerge out of email blasts and membership rosters. The binding DNA of any community is found in its relationships. God to Moses, Moses to Aaron, Aaron to the people. One relationship at a time, each important unto itself, and in the hands of a skilled community organizer, the social capital necessary if you want anything to happen.

And, sure enough, the central issue emerges. On the surface, it is to transform a people from slavery to freedom, from Egypt to the land flowing with milk and honey, from serving Pharaoh to serving God. But at its core, the nub of our drama is found in God's ability to convince Moses, and Moses' ability to convince Israel, of the most important distinction of all: the gap between the world as it is and the world as it ought to be. Over and over and over again, Moses impresses on the people the importance of looking forward and not back. It is, in a sense, the corollary to empathy not only to identify with the plight of another person, but to inspire that person (or people) to the realization that the world in which we live in today need not be the world of tomorrow. This is the prophetic litmus test for any organizer past, present, and future: the ability to articulate a compelling vision of how the world ought to be.

It is here that we get to the heart of this week's Torah reading: the plague cycle, in which Moses the revolutionary, an organizer and agitator, brings the wrath of God upon the house of Pharaoh. On a fairly obvious level, the plagues follow all of Alinsky's "Rules for Radicals." Tactically, they shift the terms of the debate: the condition of the Israelites is no longer just Moses' problem but the problem of all of Egypt. Moses hits the Egyptians hard – the Nile, livestock, the firstborn – at the heart of Pharaoh's interests. The plagues demonstrate that Moses is a leader who can bring results. Their rhythmic quality, one after the other, keeps the pressure on. Time and again Moses shows not only that he can bring a plague, but that he can also end a plague, a skill that strikes me as equally important. And the power of the plagues is not just their intensity, but their number. We know there are ten plagues; Pharaoh does not. In Alinsky's words: "Power is not what you have, but what the enemy thinks you have." Right now Moses is perceived as the man with an endless number of arrows in his quiver. The plagues create an unstable and, in Pharaoh's mind, unsustainable situation in which the Egyptian people have turned against their leader, a circumstance that we know will soon lead to Pharaoh's capitulation to the demands on the table.

As is often noted, the intended audience of the plagues was not just Pharaoh and not just the Egyptians, but the children of Israel themselves. This was an extended trust-building exercise with the Israelites. The plagues established God's relationship to Moses and Moses' relationship to the people. Strange as it sounds, the plagues were not only to antagonize, but to secure a base, the all-important relationship between God and Moses and Israel.

And because there were not one or three or five, but ten plagues, we learn another critical principle of community organizing: stamina. This is a campaign that does not take place overnight. It is a test of wills, a contest over who will blink first. Perhaps the most elusive element of organizing is the ingredient of staying power – the ability of a person, a committee or a community to identify an ideal, nurture it, develop it, fight for it, in thick and thin over a sustained amount of time. Pharaoh's heart may have hardened, but eventually Moses broke his will. It was Moses' stamina and perseverance that would win the day.

Finally, and perhaps most importantly, as the plague narrative wraps up in next week's Torah reading, there is an instructive scene in which Moses attributes the entire drama of the preceding chapters to God. Glossing over his own role, Moses tells the Israelites that when their children ask about the Exodus, they should say that God did it. This humility, we know, is given annual expression in the Passover Seder, where Moses – the architect of the Exodus – is never mentioned. The organizing principle is that the most effective leader is also the one who is able to contract his ego – to do what is called in Hebrew *tzimtzum* – and to know that the cause is always more important than the credit. Leadership should always be driven by values, issues, and ideals, not by personalities. Rhetoric, reputation, charisma. We need to use every weapon in our personal arsenal to fight for what we believe in, but these are the means, not the ends. We can never let our egos obscure that it is a value, not a personality, which is at stake.

To review, here are a few leadership principles from our Torah reading:

Empathy is the beginning of organizing.

Community organizing begins with one-on-one relationships.

Always reach from the world as it is towards the world as it ought to be.

When the time comes, dramatic tactics have their place. Hit them hard, hit them repeatedly, but always make sure your base is secure.

Staying power or stamina is what separates great leaders from good ones.

Leadership is never about you but about the values that are made evident in the life of the community

There are, I am sure, many more principles to be learned from our Torah reading. For us as a community what is most important is not that we identify them, but that we infuse our community with them. Ultimately, the record of our community will be a reflection of the degree to which we give life to these themes throughout the year. We dare not let our values and ideals lie lazily on the scriptural page. As Jews, as Zionists, as New Yorkers, as global citizens, we are, without a doubt, living through a moment with historic challenges, threats, and opportunities. Not unlike King, not unlike Alinsky, not unlike Moses himself, we are faced with the question of how we will respond to the pressing issues of the day. We dare not do nothing. In a world where there are no men, may we be the men and the women that we aspire to be. May we organize in the spirit of our predecessors, defend the values we hold dear, and build a future worthy of the love that we have for our children.

A Time to Stand Down, Not Double Down

Of late, when I think of Israel's Prime Minister Bibi Netanyahu, I think of the opening scene of *La Bohème*. Puccini's famed opera begins in the home of Marcello and Rudolfo as they seek to stave off the bitter cold of winter. Desperate to stay warm but lacking the wood to maintain a fire, Rudolfo takes hold of a bulky manuscript, a drama he had written, and tosses it into the fire. Act by act, scene by scene, Rudolfo's masterpiece burns to ashes. The two men sit comforted by the warmth of the fire, a fleeting warmth that the viewing audience knows comes at the expense of the very thing actually able to lift our bohemian friends out of their desperate straits.

Ever since Prime Minister Netanyahu accepted an invitation from Representative John Boehner to speak to Congress without the blessing of President Barack Obama, American Jewry has been thrust into a terribly unfortunate and terribly uncomfortable position. Whether Prime Minister Netanyahu is acting out of principle – to urgently state his case against a nuclear Iran – or out of political expediency – to score points at home in the month prior to the Israeli election – the effect on American Jewry is one and the same. For the first time in a very long time, American Jews are being asked to choose between a visibly upset American administration and an unyielding leader of the Jewish state. In this winter run-up to the Israeli elections, is Netanyahu really tossing the sacred script of American-Israeli relations into the fire in order to score an electoral advantage? Israel does not have the luxury of picking and choosing her friends, so why in the world would she aggravate the leader of her biggest and bestest friend of all? How is it possible, we ask behind closed doors, that the Prime Minister does not understand the effect his actions have on American Jewry? After all, Mr. Prime Minister, to side with you means to side with the person who has caused offense to my president. With the stakes so high, is this really the moment you want Israel's most vocal supporters to be rendered silent for fear of choosing between impossible options?

The truth of the matter, however, is that it is not just this most recent flare-up between the Prime Minister and the President that has rankled the ranks of American Jewry. Ever since the December call for new elections, American Jewry has watched the news in Israel with great trepidation. The political climate wrought by coalition politics has served to undercut the possibility of a two-state solution anytime in the foreseeable future. To be clear, and to reiterate what I have said from this bimah before, a two-state solution can and should happen only when it does not undermine Israel's security. Israel need not make any apologies for its refusal to allow a fundamentalist Gaza-like state to emerge in the West Bank. But when Israel's settlement practices and public discourse preclude the possibility of a two-state outcome to emerge, when Israel's own policies run counter to the policies of the American administration and, for that matter, Israel's own stated positions, American Jewry is thrust into a difficult position. Imagine an electoral outcome next month in which an Israeli coalition is formed that either explicitly or implicitly disavows a two-state solution. What, I wonder, will American Jews like me do when a chasm opens up between the policies of the Israeli and American administrations? What exactly will it mean to support an Israeli government whose policies run counter to my conscience and my country?

The fault lines between Israel and diaspora Jewry, however, exist not just in the spheres of geopolitics, but at the very heart of Jewish identity. If you know a thing or two about Israel's system of coalition politics, then you also know that whoever the next Prime Minister is, odds are he or she will partner with the Ultra-Orthodox parties in order to form a governing coalition. In a story that dates back to the founding of the state itself, while the religious parties readily defer to the Prime Minister on matters of political boundaries, they do so only insofar as the Prime Minister defers to them when it comes to defining the borders of Judaism and the Jewish people. The chief rabbinate's intransigence on matters of conversion should be deeply troubling to anyone invested in global Jewish peoplehood. It would be reason enough for alarm, if it were only the case (which it is) that the conversions of Reform, Conservative, and some Orthodox American rabbis are not acknowledged by Israel. But what about the thousands of Ukrainian Jews who are contemplating imminent immigration due to political instability? Is it possible that we live in a world where a Jew flees to Israel only to discover his or her Jewishness is questioned by the Jewish state? What about the thousands of Russian immigrants already in Israel who may live in and die for the state, but cannot be married or buried by a rabbi because they are not Jewish according to the Haredi rabbinate?

It is because all matters of personal identity in Israel are in the hands of the chief rabbinate that all non-Orthodox expressions of Judaism are stymied. Not just conversion, not just marriage and burial, but government funding of educational institutions; who does and doesn't get to pray at the Western Wall; and so much more. When our congregational trips go to Israel, we are told by the hotels that we cannot pray in the hotel chapels as we do here in America. Why? Because the hotels are under the supervision of the chief rabbinate. There is a bitter irony in the realization that one of the only countries in the world where a Jew faces discrimination for how she or he practices Judaism is the Jewish state. As the politics in Israel become more fractious, not less, the stranglehold of the ultra-Orthodox community on religious life will increase, not decrease. The politicization and Haredization of the Israeli chief rabbinate is not just the concern of a few liberally minded American rabbis; it is a concern for anyone concerned about the future of the global Jewish people.

All of which, needless to say, is an altogether distressing situation. But what we need to understand, and what Israeli leadership needs to understand, is that it is a worsening state of affairs that will ultimately serve to undercut Israel's security. Why? Because if in the next election the right-wing community is further emboldened, then the vast majority of American Jewry – you and me, our children and children's children – who live and breathe a Judaism that is anything but right wing – will wake up to find ourselves alienated from the Israel we are wired to love so much. And if American Jewry finds itself disillusioned, disenfranchised, and just plain old distant from Israel, then, my friends, it is not just we who have the problem, but Israel itself. In three weeks I will be at the AIPAC conference, and I hope many of you will be there too. To what degree, I wonder, will our Congress – Republican or Democrat – care about Israel if American Jewry no longer believes itself a vested stakeholder in the destiny of the Jewish state? Make no mistake, American Jewry plays a critical role in securing Israel's position on the world stage. To the image with which we began, in this winter run-up to the election, are Israeli politicians really prepared to throw away Israel's long-term interests in order to score short-term political advantage?

Embedded in this week's Torah reading is a legal concept called *hatra'a* – roughly translating as "forewarning." Although the biblical text clearly states the concept of an eye for eye, tooth for tooth, life for life, the rabbis instituted all sorts of safeguards to minimize the possibility of capital punishment, including the obligation to give *hatra'a* – warning or caution to those about to commit a misdeed. It is a fascinating legal proviso of Jewish law that when the stakes are really high, in order for a wrongdoer to be deemed fully culpable, they must have been forewarned of the gravity of their intended deed. No different from other spheres of Jewish law, the notion of *hatra'a* suggests that guilt for wrongdoing falls not just on the wrongdoer, but also on the community at hand – who are obligated to caution a person regarding the deleterious consequences of his or her intended action. We are all, in other words, our brothers' and sisters' keepers, which is why, by extension, no Jew may ever remain silent in the face of a misdeed. One cannot ever stand idly by, especially if given the resources or the pulpit to stop a wrong in its tracks.

And neither shall I.

"For the sake of Zion I will not be silent, for the sake of Jerusalem I will not be still." (Isaiah 62:1) The temperature and tone of the conversation needs to be dialed down immediately. If Prime Minister Netanyahu is as concerned about Iran as he purports to be, as all of us in this room are, then surely he and his advisors can find a way to state the case effectively without alienating the leader of the free world. This is the time to stand down, not double down. The clarity of message regarding the Iranian threat will be less politicized – and thus delivered far more effectively – if spoken by the Israeli Prime Minister, whoever that may be, after the election, not before. As for President Obama, who patented the notion of "beer diplomacy," maybe this is the moment to drink some of his own brew. Invite the Prime Minister over, not on a state visit, with no fanfare, and show the world, to paraphrase the rabbis, that in the place where there are no men, you are the man! I have absolutely no idea what the right answer is when it comes to Iran, but I am pretty sure that the only beneficiary of the present political spectacle and debacle is the very country that we all agree sits at the heart of the problem. Support for Israel must be swiftly returned to its bipartisan status. Prime Minister Netanyahu's intended speech before Congress is wrongheaded, and it is the responsibility of American Jewry to forewarn the Prime Minister of the consequences of his intended project.

As for the elections themselves, before any ballots are cast, Israel would do well to "look long," given the stakes at hand. Are Israelis really prepared to elect a government whose policies stand at odds with world opinion, the American administration, and the vast majority of American Jewry? Only Israel can decide what is and isn't in her security interests, but for the sake of Israel's international standing, she must make clear in word and deed that the lack of progress is the fault of the Palestinians, not Israel – an effort that will only happen by way of going the extra mile towards a two-state solution. As for global Jewish identity, are Israelis really prepared to elect a government whose stance on religious matters serves to alienate the very Jews whose support it needs in Congress and beyond? The Prime Minister of Israel cannot claim to speak on behalf of world Jewry and then alienate half of that Jewry. One and only one Jew could ever claim to speak for all Jews – and that was the first one, Abraham – a state of affairs that ended the moment his wife Sarah arrived on the scene. No differently than each of us, when an Israeli goes to the polls, I imagine there are countless factors that go into choosing a candidate. May I be so bold as to suggest that one of those factors be the status of the other half of world Jewry, six million Jews who are affected by and invested in and – whether Israelis care to admit it or not – are shapers of Israel's status on the world stage.

Without a doubt, diaspora Jewry and Israel can make for strange bedfellows. We do not vote in each other's elections, our culture and concerns are far from one and the same, but by a blessed and on occasion awkward twist of fate, our destinies are tied one to the other. Like two siblings who share a family of origin yet walk this world apart, Israel and diaspora Jewry must be ever vigilant to care for each other and protect each other, to correct each other when we step out of line, and always to do so in a way that bespeaks our enduring and overriding loyalty. After all, if we can't say these things to each other with love, then who can? Let us have the dialogue that only siblings can, filled with mutual concern, acknowledging our differences, all the while gently nudging each other towards arriving safely at our shared destiny.

Terumah/Purim

European Jewry: Stay or Go?

O ur tradition teaches: *Mishenikhnas Adar marbim b'simḥah*, when [the month of] Adar enters, one must increase joy. (Babylonian Talmud, Taanit 29a) For me, as I imagine for you, it has been a difficult commandment to fulfill as we greeted this new month with a sense of gloom. No sooner had we announced the arrival of this month containing Purim, than we awoke to the news of the most recent violent incident of European anti-Semitism, a shooting at Copenhagen's Great Synagogue. We pray that the memory of Dan Uzan, the murdered synagogue security guard, be for a blessing and that his family be comforted amongst the mourners of Zion and Jerusalem.

As the Jewish world absorbed the news from Copenhagen, the remarks that Prime Minister Netanyahu delivered in the wake of the attack seem to have touched an exposed nerve in the collective Jewish psyche. "We say to Jews," Netanyahu declared, "to our brothers and sisters: Israel is your home . . . We are preparing and calling for the absorption of mass immigration from Europe. I would like to tell all European Jews and all Jews wherever they are: 'Israel is the home of every Jew.' . . . To the Jews of Europe and to the Jews of the world I say that Israel is waiting for you with open arms."

Repeating a sentiment he first expressed after last month's Paris attacks, Netanyahu's statement was understood to be a not-so-subtle warning that for European Jewry, the writing is on the wall. Copenhagen would not be the last anti-Semitic attack, and the Jewish community would do well to leave its hostile environment and come home to the Jewish homeland. With more than 7,000 French Jews having immigrated to Israel in 2014, double the number from the prior year, Netanyahu pressed forward on Sunday with a $45 million plan to encourage further aliyah from France, Belgium, and Ukraine.

Netanyahu's remarks provoked a series of rebuttals from both within and without the Jewish world. The governments of both France and Denmark affirmed the past, present, and future importance of French and Danish Jewry to their respective countries. In the words of Danish Prime Minister Helle Thorning-Schmidt, "They [the Jews] belong in Denmark. They are a strong part of our community, and we will do everything we can to protect the Jewish community in our country."

The most vociferous responses to Netanyahu's call for mass immigration, however, came from the leadership of the Jewish community. Both the French Chief Rabbi Haim Korsia and the Danish Chief Rabbi Jair Melchior expressed their disappointment with Netanyahu, with Melchior explaining, "Terror is not a reason to move to Israel . . . People from Denmark move to Israel because they love Israel, because of Zionism. If the way we deal with terror is to run somewhere else, we should all run to a deserted island." Or, in the pointed words of ADL National Director Abe Foxman: "I don't think he [Netanyahu] should urge them . . . No, I don't think we should so easily grant Hitler a posthumous victory." Should European Jewry stay or go? It is a debate that is playing out in the halls of Jewish philanthropy. Should UJA or the Jewish Agency direct resources towards supporting and protecting Jewish life in Europe or should those funds go towards facilitating the immigration of European Jewry to Israel? It is an internal Jewish debate that, prompted by the news of the past month, has spilled out into the open – a debate reflecting the angst of being a diaspora Jew.

It is also a set of circumstances that is not new. We need look no further than the scroll of this season, the book of Esther, to understand the tensions we face. In the words of the great scholar S.D. Goitein, "Esther is an Exilic book, written in the Exile, for the Exile." (*Bible Studies*, p. 62) Esther isn't the only biblical narrative to take place outside of the land of Israel, but Purim is the only Jewish holiday commemorating a victory over anti-Semitism in the diaspora. But more telling than its location are the diasporic tensions it reflects: the socio-political condition of the Jewish community of ancient Persia. "There is," explains Haman to Ahasuerus, "a nation, apart and scattered from those of every other people of your empire. Their laws are different from those of every other people, and they do not keep the king's laws. It is not in your majesty's interest to leave them alone." (Esther 3:9) In this single verse, Haman gives expression to the neurosis of diaspora Jewry. A minority population that is vulnerable to the whims of the majority population. A people who are suspected of dual loyalties and powerless to address their exposed condition. *Megillat Esther* is not overly didactic, it is supposed to feel like a fairy tale; but like all great narratives, it is filled with vexing questions. Was Esther right or wrong to hide her Jewish identity? Is the scroll's take-home message to assimilate into non-Jewish culture or to maintain boundaries between the Jews and the host population? Purim indeed celebrates a diaspora victory, but why does it do so without mention of God or a return to the land of Israel? Is its message one of hostile resistance and revenge or of accommodation? Is it a defense or a critique of diaspora life? The answers aren't clear and I don't think they are meant to be. Esther forces us to squirm on the point of these and other needling questions without offering tidy answers. But the most enduring challenge of all, the one that we have never shaken off and continue to struggle with today, is the haunting spectre of Haman. Is diaspora Jewry in a perennially contingent status, where one day it's fine and the next it's black? Is it just a matter of time before another virulent Haman-like expression of anti-Semitism rears its head and we, like the Jews of Persia, find ourselves waiting on a miracle for salvation? The book of Esther serves as a sort of anti-Semitic looking glass for every age: a wake-up call for the diaspora princess who has fallen into a terminal slumber, a condition that can only be liberated, at least in Netanyahu's mind, with the kiss of national Jewish life. (A. Shapira, *Modern Judaism*, "Anti-Semitism & Zionism," p. 231)

The intellectual pedigree of Prime Minister Netanyahu's recent remarks is not so difficult to trace. The nineteenth-century Russian Zionist thinker Leo Pinsker, in the wake of the anti-Jewish Russian pogroms of 1881, castigated his diaspora co-religionists for deluding themselves into thinking that they would one day find acceptance by their enlightened hosts. "Since the Jew is nowhere at home," wrote Pinsker, "nowhere regarded as a native, he remains an alien everywhere." Pinsker's most famous essay was entitled "Auto-emancipation," in which he argued that the *only* remedy for the diaspora Jew's degraded position was to stop depending on the good will of a host country and to create "one single refuge," a homeland of our own. And if Pinsker's language is reminiscent of Netanyahu, it may just be because it was the Prime Minister's late father, the great historian Professor Benzion Netanyahu, who, whether writing about Jewish communities of ancient Persia, fifteenth-century Spain, nineteenth-century Russia, or twentieth-century Europe, also held this lachrymose understanding of Jewish history. It is a view perhaps best summed up by the elder Netanyahu's one-time employer Ze'ev Jabotinsky, who in 1937 prophetically proclaimed to his Jewish brethren: "Eliminate the Diaspora, or the Diaspora will surely eliminate you." Important as the gravitational "pull" of the Zionist dream is for Netanyahu (both father and son), it is also the diasporic push of anti-Semitism that undoubtedly informs his vision. Proof positive is the Prime Minister's most recent campaign video in which he tells the story of his grandfather being beaten unconscious by an anti-Semitic mob in the heart of Europe. The Prime Minister shares that before passing out, his grandfather thought: "What a disgrace . . . the descendants of the Maccabees lie in the mud powerless to defend themselves." If he survived, Netanyahu's grandfather pledged, he would bring his family to Israel. At this point in the story the Prime Minister looks into the camera and says, "I am standing here today as the Prime Minister of Israel because my grandfather kept his promise." Agree or disagree, there is no denying that Netanyahu's ideological vision is remarkably coherent and consistent. It is a vision anchored in Jewish history, attuned to the present threats facing our people, and wholly invested in the future security of global Jewry.

So too, given the events of recent months, it is an assessment that cannot be ignored. As Professor Deborah Lipstadt recently wrote: "This is not another Holocaust, but it's bad enough." Being Jewish in

Manhattan is an anomaly; our present comfort is the exception, not the norm. Ours is an era where large pockets of the Jewish world, in Europe and elsewhere, live with physical insecurity. No different than the protagonists of the book of Esther, diaspora Jews are holding their breath and bracing for the next act of anti-Semitic violence. Like Esther, we appeal to gentile powers for justice, imagining our plea to have some effect, all the while aware that the forces seeking our harm grow closer and stronger. The difference, of course, between our era and that of Esther, is that we do have a home, we do have a State of Israel. Our diaspora is not one of forced exile; it is a choice that has been made. The question is not whether Netanyahu's assessment is right or wrong. Objectively, his descriptive assessment is on the mark. The only question is the prescriptive one, namely, what shall be done about it? Netanyahu's answer is mass immigration. If that is not your answer, then it is incumbent upon you, upon all of us, to secure the safety and security of our at-risk brothers and sisters scattered around the world.

The turning point of the book of Esther comes in its fourth chapter when Mordecai, aware of the gravity of the situation, pleads with Esther to intervene on behalf of the Jewish people. Esther initially demurs, to which Mordecai famously replies: "Do not imagine that you, of all the Jews, will escape with your life by being in the King's palace. On the contrary, if you keep silent in this crisis, relief and deliverance will come to the Jews from another place . . ." (4:13-14) It is Mordecai's final word – *makom*, place – that is most enigmatic and thus the subject of much debate. What exactly, the rabbis ask, is the "place" to which Mordecai was referring that could deliver Jews from their crisis? While some understand *makom* to be a veiled reference to one of God's many names, this year may I make the suggestion that Mordecai was simply giving voice to a prophetic Zionist mentality altogether applicable to our moment. In other words, you, Esther, have two choices: You can either stand up to anti-Semitism or go to a place, a Jewish homeland, in which you will find relief. It is this choice we face today. Diaspora Jewry can either stand up to the present challenges or make aliyah. To do neither, to stand idly by with Jewish lives at risk, is simply not an option. To paraphrase Mordecai: Who knows, perhaps we have attained our position for just such a crisis? May we, like Esther, rise to the challenge of the day, support global Jewry, support the Jewish state, and live to see the day, please God soon, that the Jewish people know only *orah v'simhah, sasson v'yikar*, "light and gladness, happiness and honor." (Esther 8:16)

Vayikra/Shabbat HaḤodesh
The Hidden Question

According to the Mishnah, today's arrival of the Hebrew month of Nisan signals the ascension of the kings of Israel. While it may be a bit misplaced to announce a coronation, the resounding victory of Binyamin Netanyahu in last week's elections would, at the very least, appear to be consistent with the spirit of the season. With his Likud party having won thirty seats, the formation of a ruling coalition with Netanyahu as Prime Minister appears to be all but certain.

In my mind, the most interesting thing about the election was not who won or lost, but the emergence of a different kind of dark horse, a topic that did not come to the fore until the eleventh hour: the Palestinian-Israeli conflict. Think about it. Over the past few months, throughout the entire election season, our collective attention has been focused almost entirely on one subject: Iran. How close is Iran to a bomb? Which candidate is best able to stand up to the threat? How much enriched uranium is too much? And of course, was the Prime Minister right or wrong to bring his case before the US Congress? Some attention, no question, was paid to ISIS and a host of Israeli domestic issues, but if memory serves, our attention has decidedly not been focused on comparing the relative merits of each candidate's recommendations towards resolving the Palestinian-Israeli conflict.

And then, in the final run-up to the election, the question burst forth. Netanyahu stated that a Palestinian state would never be formed on his watch, a pronouncement seemingly at odds with his 2009 Bar Ilan speech affirming a two-state solution. The location of

Netanyahu's speech, as much as the speech itself, was altogether telling: Har Homa, which, you may recall, has been ground zero on the question of settlements. So too, Netanyahu's pre-election warning that Arab voters are "streaming in huge quantities to the polling stations," was also understood as an attempt to leverage fears within the Israeli electorate that the Israeli-Arab community may displace the Jewish interests of Israel. In the days since the election, Netanyahu retracted his pre-election statements, reaffirming his support for a two-state solution. It is a fascinating turn of events. The one thing that nobody has been talking about, ultimately revealed to be the elephant in the room: the Arab population within Israel and the West Bank, the peace process, and the viability of a two-state solution. Not unlike a breakthrough in therapy, it is almost as if the election functioned to bring out the question buried deep inside Israel's psyche, the question that anyone who knows their history knows sits at the very core of Israel's soul.

As far back as 1907, the Hebrew writer Yitzhak Epstein penned an essay entitled "*Sh'eilah Ne'elamah*" – the hidden question. A pioneering Zionist, Epstein opens his essay: "Among the difficult issues regarding the rebirth of our people in its homeland, one issue outweighs them all: our relations with the Arabs." Epstein understood that alongside the demise of the Ottoman Empire and the rise of political Zionism there existed another historic current with which to contend: the Arab nationalist movement. In bringing the "hidden question" into the open, Epstein's intention was to bolster, not undercut, the Zionist cause. In his own words, "If we don't want to ruin our work, we must consider every step we take in our homeland, and we must urgently solve the question of our relations with the Arabs before it becomes a 'Jewish question.' We must not rest content with the current situation!" (*Jew in the Modern World*, pp. 631-635) For Epstein, the viability of the Jewish national project went hand-in-hand with Arab national aspirations. Not to openly contend with the "hidden question" – namely, how do we figure out all these competing claims for a single piece of land – would put the sustainability of the Zionist project itself at risk.

Epstein was not the first and certainly not the last to ask the "hidden question." A review of the last hundred-plus years of Zionist literature is peppered with examples of our greatest minds grappling with the question of this "land of two peoples." In 1891, Ahad Ha'am, the revered founder of cultural Zionism, returned from a visit to Palestine to pen an essay entitled "Truth from the Land of Israel" filled with reflections on the Arab population. Or, if you like, point to David Ben Gurion, who in a 1930 address to the World Congress for Labor Palestine in Berlin implored his comrades to pay attention to the Arab question, even "with all the discomfort that it entails for us." (Mendes-Flohr in Introduction to Buber, *A Land of Two Peoples*, p. 6) It wasn't just the political left, like the 1925 founders of Brith Shalom, who asked the question openly. As early as 1921, Ze'ev Jabotinsky, the ideological forefather of Netanyahu's Likud party, openly acknowledged the Arab national movement. To be sure, in Jabotinsky's mind, "Jewish needs" would always trump "Arab claims" (especially in the shadow of Hitler's Germany), but even Jabotinsky would acknowledge the claims of others, at the same time as he fought on behalf of his people.

So too, as the national aspirations of the Jewish people took shape, the world at large would ever seek to manage the competing claims made by these two peoples for this one land. The same 1917 Balfour declaration in which ". . . his Majesty's Government view[ed] with favour the establishment in Palestine of a national home for the Jewish people," also asserted that "nothing shall be done which may prejudice the civil and religious rights of existing non-Jewish communities in Palestine." The November 29, 1947, partition plan, likewise, sought to establish independent Arab and Jewish states side-by-side. From her very founding Israel has had to fight for her right to exist, all the while contending both internally and externally with the national narratives running parallel to her own.

These questions only became pricklier as the State of Israel went from abstraction to reality. When forced into war in 1967, Israel asserted her right to self-defense, a territorial expansion into Sinai, Gaza and the West Bank, which, whether intended, accidental, or otherwise, raised a far less hidden question: How should or shouldn't Israel engage the millions of Arab non-citizens of this territory, which to this day is neither annexed nor returned? The "hidden question" is no longer merely the question of Jews and Arabs in pre-State Palestine, not just the question of how best to integrate Israeli-Arabs into the Jewish state, but ever since 1967, the question of how Israel can remain, with its present boundaries, both a Jewish and democratic state.

To be sure, neither in 1947 nor in 1967, nor really ever, did Israel's Arab neighbors ask the question of co-existence with the same conscientiousness as did Israel. Arab and Palestinian rejection of the Jewish state has not afforded Israel the luxury of dropping her guard long enough to do more than theorize as to what peace would look like. From rejecting the partition plan, to attacking the new nation in 1948, to the three "nos" of the post-1967 Khartoum Resolution (no peace, no recognition, and no negotiations with Israel), to the Yom Kippur War, to the hundreds of rockets hurled into Israel from Gaza last summer, one cannot really blame Israel for her reticence to facilitate the creation of yet another unstable neighboring Arab country hostile to Israel's existence. Certainly, the history of Israel's withdrawals from Southern Lebanon in 2000 and Gaza in 2006, which were both followed not by peace but by rockets, should give pause to any Israeli government thinking of doing the same in the West Bank. When Israel's so-called partners are not even prepared to acknowledge her right to exist, even the most left-leaning supporters of Israel are at a loss to identify who it is exactly with whom Israel should be making peace.

There is no crisp answer to the "Hidden Question." If there were, we wouldn't still be asking it over one hundred years later. But even without an answer we need to keep asking the question, we need to do so publicly, and we need to expect our leaders to do the same. Of all the sacrificial offerings described in today's Torah reading, the most interesting by far is the one offered by the Israelite chieftain who, upon being informed of a misdeed, publicly acknowledges it with a sin offering. Rabbi Yochanan Ben Zakkai praises the good fortune of a people with such a leader. Why? Because in taking on personal agency to meet the exigencies of the hour, that leader inspires a generation to do the same. A true leader does not duck, dodge, or deny; a true leader does not sweep things under the rug or kick the can down the road. Neither our concerns regarding Iran and ISIS nor the painful shortcomings of the Palestinian leadership gives us a pass to avoid addressing the Palestinian-Israeli conflict. The Israeli electorate has spoken, and it is incumbent upon the next Israeli government to nurture the conditions by which coexistence for these two people with one land can one day emerge. The test of Netanyahu's leadership is not whether he does or doesn't solve the conflict, nor for that matter, whether you, I, or President Obama agrees with how he chooses to do so. The test for Netanyahu will be found, no differently than for the Israelite chieftain of old, in his ability to publicly name the challenge of the hour, articulate a vision moving forward, summon the political courage to act on it, and sustain that effort through thick and thin. It is not just for the Palestinian future that we work towards a solution, but rather for the future of a secure, Jewish, and democratic State of Israel. If, as it seems at the moment, the election has served to turn our attention to the Israeli-Palestinian conflict, then no matter what your personal politics may be, that is something we can all be pleased and hopeful about.

At the conclusion of every Jewish wedding ceremony, the seventh and final wedding blessing asks God to speedily restore to the cities of Judah and the outskirts of Jerusalem, the voices of bridegroom and bride, of joy and gladness, of young people feasting and singing – a hope that has been, time and again, shattered like the broken glass itself. Neither joy and gladness nor peace and security have arrived in the cities of Judah and outskirts of Jerusalem. Despite the failures of past generations, we must, nevertheless, try, try again. The alternative is just too awful to consider. We must look for every opportunity to draw this conflict to an end, and we must do so before any further windows of opportunity close. As Rabbi Tarfon taught: "It is not incumbent upon us to complete the work, but neither are we at liberty to desist from it." (*Pirkei Avot* 2:1) May the democratically elected leadership of Israel find the courage to ask all the uncomfortable hidden questions, may our would-be partners do the same, and may we all press forward pursuing peace, building a future filled with Hebrew and Arabic shouts of joy and gladness, a future that we all so desperately want and need.

Shabbat HaGadol/Parashat Tzav
Freedom's Journey

When Generals Robert E. Lee and Ulysses S. Grant sat down together at Appomattox in April 1865, an exchange of their respective Seder plans was not high on their list of priorities. And yet, one hundred and fifty years since the end of the Civil War, it is altogether remarkable to realize that the surrender of the Confederate forces to the Union took place on the eve of the Jewish festival of freedom. On this Shabbat HaGadol, as we prepare for both our upcoming seders and the sesquicentennial observance of that historic day, it strikes me as an opportune time not only to consider the significance of April 1865 in our nation's history, but also to reflect on how that historical pivot continues to shape the landscape of our country through this very day.

Although any schoolchild will tell you that 1776 was the year our nation was founded, 1865 was arguably the first opportunity for the ideals embedded in the Declaration of Independence to be given full expression.

> "We hold these truths to be self-evident, that all men are created equal, that they are endowed by their Creator with certain unalienable Rights, that among these are Life, Liberty and the pursuit of Happiness."

Familiar as we are with Jefferson's words, we are also undoubtedly aware that Jefferson, Washington, Madison, and Monroe, among other Founding Fathers, were slaveholders. To be sure, Jefferson's initial draft of the Declaration did contain a denunciation of slavery, a passage that was excised at the urging of delegates from South Carolina and Georgia. Nevertheless, be it Jefferson's ownership of slaves, his reflections on Negro inferiority in his celebrated *Notes on Virginia*, or his reticence to address the issue of slavery head on, an honest assessment of our nation's founding must at some point confront the moral paradox built into the establishment of our "almost-chosen" nation. As with so many leaders, past and present, Jefferson and his contemporaries kicked the can of this quandary down the road. In Jefferson's own words, "It is to them I look, to the rising generations, and not to the one now in power for these great reformations." (David Brion Davis, *The Problem of Slavery in the Age of Emancipation*, pp. 177-8)

The boiling point would come with the Civil War. By this telling, it would be the shots fired at Fort Sumter in 1861, and not the ones at Lexington in 1775 that served as the birth pangs of our nation.

> "Four score and seven years ago our fathers brought forth on this continent, a new nation, conceived in Liberty, and dedicated to the proposition that all men are created equal."

Ostensibly, Lincoln's Gettysburg Address served to dedicate a cemetery and honor those felled in battle, but what Lincoln understood better than anyone was that his dedication was aimed not only to the memory of the fallen soldiers of Gettysburg, but to the vision of the Founding Fathers: "a government of the people, by the people, for the people." Gettysburg would serve as the political and ideological tipping point from which Lincoln could issue the Emancipation Proclamation just a few months later on January 1, 1863. Of course, even then it would take nearly eighteen months and thousands of American lives before the fighting would come to an end. The fight was hard fought. As Lincoln intoned in his second inaugural, both sides – the abolitionists and the apologists for slavery – "read the same Bible and pray[ed] to the same God," dividing the nation not just by geography or interpretation of the Constitution, but by the interpretation of sacred scripture itself. Just over one month after his national call to "finish the work we are in," just six days after the surrender of General Lee to Grant, on Shabbat, April 15, 1865, Lincoln would die by an assassin's bullet, having seen, but not yet entered, the Promised Land.

At the risk of stating the obvious, the end of the Civil War did not draw our nation's struggle for freedom to a close. In the words of Fredrick Douglass: "Verily, the work does not end with the abolition of slavery, but only begins." For both sides, "postwar reconstruction would prove to be a painful, slow and flawed, nightmare." For the newly emancipated African-American community, the coming years would be marked by "ambiguity, tragedy and complexity." (Jay Winik, *April 1865*, p. 381) As for white America – old hatreds, as the saying goes, die hard. It is far from a coincidence that the Ku Klux Klan would be founded in the year following the Civil War. Most of all, as Jay Winik explains in his study on the subject, it would be the world of race relations that would continue to suffer. In state after state, restrictive legislation regarding segregation, intermarriage, land ownership, voting rights, and countless other forms of racial repression would continue to dominate the American landscape. Not unlike our Passover story, the generation of the Exodus would not necessarily be the generation able to fully enjoy the taste of freedom.

All of which, I am sure, was not lost on Martin Luther King, Jr. as he sat in the Birmingham jail on that Passover day of 1963. In a passage that could have just have easily been written by Moses himself, King wrote: "We know through painful experience that freedom is never voluntarily given by the oppressor; it must be demanded by the oppressed." The brilliance of King's rhetoric of civil rights was that he positioned his cause not as something new or revolutionary, but as the logical and necessary fulfillment of Lincoln's vision. It was no accident that just a few months after Birmingham, in the shadow of the Lincoln Memorial, King began his "I have a Dream Speech" with the words "Five score years ago."

> "In a sense," King declared . . . "We've come to our nation's capital to cash a check. When the architects of our republic wrote the magnificent words of the Constitution and the Declaration of Independence, they were signing a promissory note to which every American was to fall heir. This note was a promise that all men, yes, black men as well as white men, would be guaranteed the 'unalienable Rights' of 'Life, Liberty and the pursuit of Happiness.' It is obvious today that Amer-

ica has defaulted on this promissory note, insofar as her citizens of color are concerned."

From Brown vs. Board of Education to Rosa Parks to sit-ins and marches, every aspect of the Civil Rights movement leading up to the Civil Rights Act of 1964 outlawing discrimination based on race, color, religion, sex, or national origin, was an effort to fulfill the vision expressed, but not realized, by Jefferson. The Civil Rights Act itself would not mark the end of the journey, but just another step along the way. Just a few weeks ago, our nation observed the 50th anniversary of Bloody Sunday – March 7, 1965 – when a peaceful protest march from Selma to Montgomery sought to cross the Edmund Pettus Bridge, which whether out of irony or intent, was named after a past Confederate soldier and Grand Dragon of the Klan. Not unlike Lincoln and altogether like Moses, having reached the mountaintop, King would not enter the Promised Land.

All of which brings us to our present day. It is April 2015, one hundred and fifty years after Appomattox, fifty years after Selma, and a week before Passover. Passover calls on us to reflect not just on the Jewish journey to freedom, but on the struggles of those still seeking to realize the biblical vision of the founding document of the Jewish people, a humanity created in the image of God, granted equal and infinite dignity regardless of race, religion, gender, or sexual orientation. One need not look very far to know that we have yet to realize the expressed visions of the Bible and the Declaration of Independence. The events of Ferguson, Staten Island, Cleveland, and beyond make it abundantly clear that insofar as citizens of color are concerned, "we must continue to strive to finish the work we are in." In the next few days, I will send an email and post on the synagogue website a haggadah supplement for you to use at your seder. I encourage you to print it out and let it shape the discussions of your seders. Try to identify the pockets of injustice and inequality that remain on the American landscape, and most importantly, commit yourself to the work yet to be done. It is neither the antebellum South, nor the 1960s – for that we can all be grateful. Though faded, the stain of our nation's founding, nevertheless, remains. It will only be by way of sustained vigilance and activism of our generation and the generations to come that we will live to see it cleansed.

Or, better yet, in the recent words of our President at Selma:

"Fifty years from Bloody Sunday, our march is not yet finished, but we're getting closer. Two hundred and thirty-nine years after this nation's founding our union is not yet perfect, but we are getting closer. Our job's easier because somebody already got us through that first mile. Somebody already got us over that bridge. When it feels the road is too hard, when the torch we've been passed feels too heavy, we will remember these early travelers, and draw strength from their example, and hold firmly the words of the prophet Isaiah: 'Those who hope in the Lord will renew their strength. They will soar on [the] wings like eagles. They will run and not grow weary. They will walk and not be faint.'

We honor those who walked so we could run. We must run so our children soar. And we will not grow weary. For we believe in the power of an awesome God, and we believe in this country's sacred promise.

May He bless those warriors of justice no longer with us, and bless the United States of America."

And may each and every one of us, enjoy a happy, healthy, and kosher Passover!

Turn to page 119 to see "Four Cups of Freedom: A Haggadah Supplement on the Occasion of the 150th Anniversary of the End of the American Civil War."

Parashat Sh'mini/Yom HaAtzma'ut
Destiny Knocking

On April 15, 1956, which was *Yom HaAtzma'ut*, Israeli Independence Day, the outlook for the young State of Israel did not look good – not good at all. In the fall of 1955, Egypt, under Gamel Abdul Nasser, had begun to orchestrate a series of guerilla attacks, to which Israel's Prime Minister, David Ben Gurion, responded with a series of counterattacks. War seemed inevitable. With tensions escalating, Ben Gurion warned on that very April day that "the Egyptians were planning 'to slaughter' them and vowed that Israel would retaliate two blows to one." (JJ Schacter, *Tradition*, 39:3).

As far as American foreign policy was concerned, the attitude of the Eisenhower administration was frosty compared to that of Truman who, you may recall, in 1948 recognized the new state eleven minutes after its founding. The State Department under Secretary of State Dulles sought to strengthen America's standing among the Arab nations and to bring Egypt out of the Soviet orbit. America repeatedly refused Israeli requests for help in obtaining nuclear capability and, for that matter, any requests for arms. Given the perceived Arab role in containing communism, the importance of Arab oil, and a general detachment or even antipathy to the Zionist cause, Israel was understood not as an ally but as an impediment to American interests.

For the pro-Israel camp, as Steven Spiegel explains in his book on the subject, the Eisenhower years were not our finest hour. Rumors floated that the administration intended to investigate the American Zionist Council, an atmosphere that prompted the formation of an independent lobbying group – what we now know as AIPAC. As for

American Jewry, we were in disarray. The administration became so frustrated with so many representatives claiming to speak for the Jewish community, that Assistant Secretary of State Henry Byroade insisted that he see them all at one time in one group, thus indirectly forming what we now know as the Conference of Presidents of Major American Jewish Organizations. (*The Other Arab-Israeli Conflict*, pp. 50-61)

As for the Orthodox community, active efforts towards securing Israel's safety were few and far between. Perhaps due to the recent trauma of the Shoah, perhaps due to an unwillingness to collaborate with the non-observant community, perhaps due to a continued reticence to acknowledge the legitimacy of the State of Israel before the advent of the Messiah – or more likely, due to a combination of all three – political, philanthropic, and institutional support for the new state was not forthcoming.

This was the situation on that Yom HaAtzma'ut of 1956. Expansionist and hostile Arab regimes, a young state under siege against threats both big and small, an Israel increasingly isolated on the world stage, an American administration at best unsympathetic to Israel, and an American Jewry that was either unable or unwilling to articulate a clear, forceful, and actionable agenda towards strengthening the case for Israel in the public sphere. The situation was not good – not good at all.

Against this historical backdrop, Rabbi Joseph Soloveitchik delivered on that April day a breathtaking lecture at Yeshiva University in honor of the eighth anniversary of the founding of the state. The lecture is titled *Kol Dodi Dofek*, "The Voice of My Beloved Knocks," a phrase taken from the fifth chapter of the biblical Song of Songs. It is easily found, not very long, and I encourage you to read it in full. Rabbi Soloveitchik, often referred to as "the Rav," is regarded as the leading Orthodox thinker of the twentieth century, his presence having shaped generations of American rabbinical leadership. At the most basic level, Soloveitchik formulates a powerful argument for the obligations of diaspora Jewry vis-à-vis Israel. In his assessment of his community's support for the settlement and building up of the land, Soloveitchik states: "We have been remiss, and our guilt is great . . .

But why should we search out the faults of others and seek to place the blame on the shoulders of secular Jews? Let us examine our own flaws and repent our sins." (*Fate and Destiny*, p. 36) Referring to the Shulamite maiden of the Song who, despite being drunk with love and yearning, fails to rise to the voice of her beloved when he comes knocking, Soloveitchik enumerates the multiple knocks, six in all, to which diaspora Jewry has failed to respond. The "knock" of the establishment of the state, the "knock" of the victory of the Israeli army over their foes, the "knock" of Jews being able for the first time in our history to defend – and if necessary, avenge – Jewish blood. So many signs, so many "knocks," and yet, the "maiden" – the religious Jewish community – fails to rise, literally and figuratively, to open to door to let in her beloved destiny of Israel. Soloveitchik castigates his community for being miserly in demeanor and in pocketbook, for failing "to exercise the proper influence on Jewish life here [in America] and on events in the land of Israel." (p. 39) Not only, Soloveitchik argued, must his community be unflinching in their support for Israel, but they must, despite profound differences with the secular community, find common cause and work together when it comes to securing Israel's future. Soloveitchik's speech was a turning point – a pivot for the religious Zionist community and perhaps for American Jewry as a whole – from a lukewarm, incoherent, and often divisive communal posture to a stance in service to a good much greater than the parochial interests of any one segment of the Jewish community.

And were it the case that Soloveitchik accomplished only that with this lecture, we could say – as the song goes – *dayenu*, that would have been enough. In my mind, however, it is a theological distinction that Soloveitchik makes towards the beginning of the lecture that is the key to it all. In confronting the horrors of Holocaust, Soloveitchik asks the question of why suffering exists; how is it possible that God could have allowed such trauma to befall the Jewish people? But unlike so many other theologians, Soloveitchik concedes that the answer to the question of suffering lies beyond human comprehension. Nevertheless, despite the lack of answers, we cannot be immobilized. We cannot be what he calls a people of fate – passive participants in the unfolding of history – much in the same way that Aaron, despite the senseless loss of his two sons in this morning's *parashah*, must move forward. The Jewish people, he explains, must move forward from their pain and understand themselves to be a people of destiny – deliberately and consciously charting out a future. We will, in all likelihood, never understand the reason for our afflictions, be they personal or national. But we can, if we so choose, recognize the blessings, the *ḥesed*, in our lives and in doing so, leverage those blessings towards strengthening the Jewish people, the State of Israel, and the world in which we live. Israel is neither a byproduct of the Holocaust, nor for that matter does her existence mitigate the trauma suffered by the Jewish people. Rather Israel embodies the unprecedented opportunity for the Jewish people to author their own narrative and become – as Professor Ken Stein teaches – the subject of our own sentence and not the object of someone else's.

Just days ago, our community observed *Yom HaShoah* and in just a few short days we will gather to celebrate *Yom HaAtzma'ut*. While loose parallels exist, we must be careful about drawing too close a correspondence between our moment and that of 1956. As Mark Twain once said, "History doesn't repeat itself, but it does rhyme." And yet, I am in agreement with my teacher Rabbi Jacob J. Schacter who observed that none of Soloveitchik's fundamental positions are in need of being reworked, "only more fully understood." (*Tradition* 39:3, p. 55) Could it not be said that our age, our moment of American Jewry, is also in desperate need of a forceful, coherent, and actionable stance when it comes to Israel's security? Are we ourselves not in danger of the emergence of – if we are not already experiencing – a chasm growing between American foreign policy interests and the interests and needs of the State of Israel? Are we not bearing witness in our day, as Soloveitchik did in his, to a widening gap between the diaspora and Israeli Jewry? Are we ourselves not guilty of letting the internal divisions of the Jewish people spill out into the open and thus undercut not only any semblance of Jewish unity, but our very ability to defend Israel effectively in her hour of need? Friends, we too are living through a turning point. Not decades from now, not years from now, but much, much sooner than any of us think, history will judge us and it will be the declarations, decisions, and deeds to which we here in this room commit that will determine not just the judgments of history, but the very future of our people.

So let us resolve here today not to be a people of fate, but to be a people of destiny. When it comes to Israel, the most strident voices are not necessarily the sane ones. Let's model a community that is capable of standing with Israel, in thick and thin, left and right, Democrat and Republican. There are those in the community, filling my inbox and yours, who would have you believe that one cannot support the New Israel Fund and AIPAC in one breath and with one checkbook, as if seeding Jewish-Arab coexistence and advocating on behalf of Israel are somehow at odds with each other. There are those who would choose to turn New York's annual Celebrate Israel parade into a circus of dissent rather than a display of Jewish unity. We here at Park Avenue Synagogue have the opportunity and, quite frankly, the heft, to demonstrate to the world that one can defend Israel in the public sphere, advocate for a two-state solution, and work towards a pluralistic vision of global Jewish peoplehood and see these goals as interdependent, not contradictory. After all, what is it we are all seeking, if not a safe, secure, Israel, peaceably co-existing with her neighbors, central to the identity of world Jewry, a world Jewry who are assured that their Jewishness is recognized and at home in the Jewish homeland? Is that vision a distant one? Undoubtedly. Are there differences in tactics and outcomes? You bet. But it would be a *shanda* of generational proportions if we in this room sat out this round of Jewish history because we were worried about those who would seek to divide us even further. It is a strange thing to advocate for, but when it comes to Israel, ours is an era in desperate need of the emergence of a sane center, a center with enough elasticity to house dissent, a center that is always able to work together in spite of our differences. This is what it means to be a people of destiny, to step up to the needs of the hour, to know that what we share far outweighs what we don't, and to fulfill our obligation to direct the blessings, the *ḥesed*, of our lives towards strengthening the Jewish people and the Jewish state.

The final paragraph of Soloveitchik's essay states the following: "Judaism has always believed . . . that a person has the ability to take his fate into his hands to mold it into destiny, into a life of freedom, meaning, and joy, that he has the power to transform isolation into solitude, a sense of inferiority into a feeling of worth." (p. 73) At the crossing of the sea, at the base of Mount Sinai, at Independence Hall in Tel Aviv in 1948, in the crisis of 1956, at every juncture of Israel's history, our people's finest hours have occurred when we have declared *na'aseh v'nishma*, we will do and we will listen, we will mold our destiny, we will live purposefully, we will author our narrative, and we will leverage the blessings of our lives for the greater good of our people. So, too, may it be in our day. May this be our prayer, may this be our mission, and may this be our continued and shared destiny.

Emor
Two Worlds of Judaism

As Israel's governing coalition was cobbled together late Wednesday night, just two hours before deadline, I thought of Winston Churchill's quip: "Democracy is the worst form of government, except for all the others." Despite the fact that Prime Minister Netanyahu won a stunning thirty-seat victory for his Likud Party, by Wednesday night his Knesset majority stood at a razor thin sixty-one seats. For those unfamiliar with the structure of Israel's 120-seat parliamentary system, the stability of any government is contingent on it having the sixty-one votes necessary to pass legislation. And because no single party in Israel's government can muster a majority on its own, the larger party (in this case Likud) offers all sorts of concessions, promises, and government portfolios to the smaller parties in order to ensure their cooperation in forwarding the larger party's agenda. Unlike the public posturing of the election season, or the acrimonious debates on the Knesset floor, it is the closed-door coalition dealings of the last forty-plus days that often set the tone and agenda of the incoming government. Who will control the education ministry – someone with a secular or a religious agenda? Who will represent Israel in foreign affairs or in negotiations with the Palestinians? That, too, is negotiated during this period. Will the minister of housing or agriculture look to secure Israel's foothold in the West Bank? These and so many other decisions shaping the future of the Jewish state were locked into place these past few days.

While we could turn our attention to the peace process, foreign policy, or any number of domestic issues Israel faces, this morning I want to address the issue that most affects North American Jewry, and that is the religious leanings of this new government. The turnaround from the last government is jarring. The deals that Prime Minister Netanyahu has made with the ultra-Orthodox party United Torah Judaism, the Sephardic ultra-Orthodox party Shas, and Naftali Bennett's Jewish Home Party have resulted in a decidedly rightward shift in this new coalition. Millions, if not billions, have been promised to ultra-Orthodox education and religious institutions. Whatever the recent rise in employment among ultra-Orthodox men may be, about 45% at last count, a series of entitlements will be set in motion incentivizing them to stay in the yeshiva and out the workforce. Legislative advances made in the past administration seeking to include the Haredi community in Israel's national military service will most certainly be rolled back. The Religious Affairs Ministry, which controls the Chief Rabbinate and its appointment processes, now sits in the hands of Shas. The past government's allowance to permit municipal Orthodox rabbis to perform conversions will most likely be rescinded. It goes without saying that any gestures towards a pluralistic vision of Israeli Jewish life have been rendered stillborn in this new coalition.

The list goes on and on, and the particulars of every deal are yet to be known. What is clear is that there has been a dramatic turnabout, as all matters of personal status have shifted into the hands of right-wing religious parties. It is not, to be sure, the first time this has happened. In fact, ever since Ben-Gurion established his first government, matters of religious concern have reflected the sensibilities of the religious right and not the Israeli electorate as a whole. Nor, for that matter, is this new state of affairs necessarily a reflection of Netanyahu himself, for whom these concessions undoubtedly reflect political expediency, not his own ideological preference. And yet, because his majority is so slim, because it would take but one of these parties leaving the coalition to force another election, the Prime Minister has been rendered totally beholden to their agendas, whose influence now extends well beyond whatever their numbers merit.

All of which, for those of us invested in the relationship between diaspora Jewry and Israel, should be a matter of major concern.

Over the last few months, I have had the honor of participating in something called the Jewish Religious Equality Coalition, a leadership group convened by the American Jewish Committee (AJC) representing the spectrum of American religious life, as well as communal heavyweights like the ADL, UJA-Federation, and others. What became clear in our meeting last week was that the religious vector of this new government – specifically, the exclusive control of the Chief Rabbinate over matters of personal status – risks severing the bond between Israel and the global Jewish people. It is not merely an internal Israeli issue: whether buses do or don't run on Shabbat, the ability of Israelis to marry outside the Orthodox rabbinate, or the hundreds of thousands of Israelis not considered Jewish by the Chief Rabbinate. The stakes extend into our lives as American Jews. Is the Judaism that is practiced and preached here recognized as Judaism? Are marriages performed outside of the Orthodox rabbinate considered marriages? Are non-Orthodox converts, their children and grandchildren considered Jews at all? With the boundaries of Jewish identity being determined by Israel's religious right, it is altogether likely – if it is not already the case – that no matter how profound our love for Israel, you and I, our Judaism will not be recognized by Israel as Jewish at all.

I fear we are living through a time when a parting of ways is taking place between American Jewry and Judaism as defined by the State of Israel. In Israel there is a tightening of definitions as to who is and isn't a Jew. Perhaps due to a fear of secularism, perhaps due to an emboldened and growing Haredi population, a strain of fundamentalism has emerged in the ultra-Orthodox community. The fences are getting higher, the requirements for conversion more stringent, and the ability of the ultra-Orthodox to countenance alternate expressions of Jewish life less and less. Like any radical religious movement, the ultra-Orthodox presume not only that they possess the sole authentic expression of faith, but also that their expression is definitive for all others.

Here in America, we are headed in the opposite direction. As evidenced by last year's Pew report, American Jewry is undergoing a process of redefinition in which the lines between Jew and non-Jew are becoming increasingly blurred. With over seventy percent of non-Orthodox Jews marrying someone born of another faith, the American rabbinate is searching for a tactical response attuned both to the tradition *and* the realities on the ground. Some of my colleagues, for instance, are pushing if not breaking the boundaries regarding intermarriage. Others, myself included, are seeking to articulate a language and practice of inclusion that embraces the would-be Jew and stretches conversion standards within the boundaries of Jewish law. We may differ in particulars, but the conditions to which we are responding are the same. Namely, how shall the American rabbinate best strengthen the increasingly heterogeneous Jewry that we have been tasked to serve? And because America, unlike Israel, ensures a separation of church and state and eschews any notion of a centralized rabbinate, the diversity of responses will undoubtedly increase in the years ahead.

This is the picture: Israeli Jewry and American Jewry are on two very different trajectories. Israel is headed towards centralization, exclusion, and insularity; American Jewry, towards decentralization, inclusion, and pluralism. Difficult as the news of this new government may be for those invested in religious pluralism, it is really just a particularly stark manifestation of a long-brewing circumstance. An Israeli journalist friend of mine sought to console me this week with the insight that this new government may prove to lack both the consensus and the longevity to do much damage on the issues we care about. Nevertheless, if we do care about the relationship between Israel and diaspora Jewry, we must do what we can, intervene where we can, in order to steer our worlds of Judaism closer. Our decision not to live in Israel precludes us from having a vote or voice in the math of Israel's Knesset. But we can and we must signal to Israel's elected leadership that our support for Israel emerges by way of our Jewish identity, a Jewish identity that must be recognized by the country we so love. We can and must support those like-minded organizations like the Conservative Movement/Masorti in Israel (www.masorti.org), like Rabbis for Religious Freedom and Equality in Israel (http://hiddush.org), and like the AJC with its recent forays into this subject (www.ajc.org). We can and must both pick fights and plant seeds, leverage all the tools at our disposal to ensure that Israel's religious future is one that is not only recognizable to American Jewry, but recognizes American Jewry as part of the global Jewish family.

At the conclusion of our Torah reading, there is an account of a troubling incident in which a man born of an Israelite mother and an Egyptian father comes to blows with a full-blooded Israelite, blasphemes God's name, and is put to death. More often than not, this incident is understood as a lesson regarding the offense of blasphemy and the collective responsibility of the community to root out such a sinner. Notwithstanding the transgression at hand, I cannot help but wonder if this entire story would have turned out differently had the Israelite community sought to integrate, not alienate, this individual on the communal fringe. Had the communal impulse been one of inclusion, not exclusion, would our sinner have been reduced to pain, anger, and rage? I don't read this tale as a lesson on the sin of blasphemy; I read it as an object lesson regarding Israel's systemic failure to countenance the diversity in its midst.

Long before this recent election and last year's Pew study, our Jewish family has wrestled with the boundaries of Jewish identity. Who is and who isn't a Jew? Who gets to decide, and what shall our posture be towards those seeking entry? May we be the generation that chooses the path of inclusion, stretching the bounds of Jewish law to extend our Jewish tent far and wide. May we support the efforts of those in Israel seeking to do the same, and may the bonds between American Jewry and Israel be healed and strengthened towards a bright future.

Shavuot
The Image Within

In relating the story of creation, the rabbis tell of God's plan to create humanity in the divine image. Having heard God's intent, the angels grew jealous and sought to foil God's plan by hiding God's image from humanity. One angel suggested that God's image be hidden at the bottom of the sea, where no person will ever find it. Another angel countered that God's image should be placed at the top of the highest mountain peak, safe from prying humankind. Hearing these ideas, the wisest of angels responded: "There may come a day that humans learn to plumb the depths of the deepest ocean. So too, humans may learn to climb the highest mountain. So let us hide God's image in the safest place of all; let us place it within the human soul itself, for that is the one place that they will never think to look."

It is a religious insight of the highest order to realize that the very thing for which we search throughout our lives is, all the while, embedded within us. From the moment Adam and Eve left the garden, through the wilderness wanderings of the Israelites, the tale of our people has been a perpetual search for a truth, an Eden, a promised land – ever elusive – existing just beyond our grasp. And like the man in the Hasidic fable who travels the world seeking a treasure that he ultimately discovers buried beneath his own home, we find that the prize we seek most is not to be found by way of some unknown frontier, but rather by way of a journey inward. Within each of us sits our better self, our higher purpose, and our inner truth. We exist in a state of self-alienation, strangers to our very selves. We live our lives seeking to be like someone else, like this one or that one, forgetting that in the final accounting the question we will be asked is not whether we were Moses, Abraham, or Sarah, but whether we were that one person we were actually created to be. The most rewarding and adventurous and arduous and necessary spiritual pilgrimage a person can make is that of self-discovery. As Hermann Hesse wrote: "Each person [has] only one vocation – to find the way to himself."

Tonight's festival of Shavuot celebrates God's revelation at Mount Sinai and the opportunity for each and every one of us to hear God's voice and reaffirm our commitment to a life of mitzvot. The conventional image is top down, a booming voice from the heavens, followed and filled by God's commandments. And yet an alternative and equally authoritative midrash suggests otherwise: that not the entire Torah, not the 613 commandments, not even the Ten Commandments were given by God at Mount Sinai. This midrash explains that only the first sound – the first vowel of the first word of the first commandment – was spoken by God, an utterance to which the entire Israelite community responded with the full content of what we know as Torah. By this telling, God's revelation was not top down. It was akin to, if not exactly like, the parent's approach to the fourth child at the seder table, the one who knows not even how to ask. *At p'tach lo,* "You shall open that child." The parent's obligation is not to pour in content, but to prompt that child to find his or her voice in the narrative of our people. Under this formulation, a life of Torah is a process of self-actualization, an articulation of the "Torah within." The revelation we celebrate today is thus self-revelation – an opportunity to give full voice to the sounds of Sinai as spoken by Israel on this very day, so many years ago.

If this is so, if the human condition is one of self-alienation, and revelation is but the opportunity to hear the voice of God within each of us, then the true nature of religious longing snaps into place. First and foremost is music. There is a sublime feeling that I hope we can all reference, whereby the combination of words, melody, and the cantor's voice tap into the *pintele yid* within each of us, cracking open our souls to release the song of our hearts. It could be the first time or the fiftieth time we have heard a prayer. What a feeling it is, when a *hazzan* is able to give expression to another place – a place within our hearts and souls – as our voices are stirred and unlocked.

So too with words of Torah. The secret of a great sermon is that the listener should not feel they are being told something new, rather that the preacher has given voice to a truth that we have known all along to be the case but have never had the courage or the tools to articulate. We all have had such an experience, when a rabbi has been speaking of Israel or Torah or the human condition, and we feel like we are being spoken to directly. "How did the rabbi know," we wonder, "what is going on in my life?" And in that moment, that rabbi has fulfilled his or her task of religious leadership, not telling us something new, but drawing out the "Torah within," the Torah that we knew all along.

Of late, I have thought long and hard about the vocation of religious leadership. I am increasingly of the opinion that the role of clergy or any Jewish educator is a form of spiritual mentoring. From a parenting perspective and from a managerial perspective, I am totally convinced of this. Lives can be molded, skills can be honed, and we are all ever works in progress, but the great "win" we seek is that those around us are nurtured and nudged forward in their quest towards finding the best version of their true selves. One cannot seek to make anyone – a child, an employee, or a student – someone they are not. Such a project will inevitably lead to failure and frustration on both sides. The task of religious mentoring is one of empowerment towards the goal of self-actualization. To help an individual find the keys to his or her own soul, to find that image of God implanted deep within, and let that person give expression to his or her distinctive voice amidst the chorus of humanity.

Cantor Ben Ellerin and Rabbi Leah Loeterman, to the degree that Cantor Schwartz and I have been able, we have sought to provide each of you with a road map to your best selves, now newly ordained clergy for the Jewish people. You have served our community with distinction as interns, and on behalf of the entire congregation, we thank you, applaud your contributions, and wish you every success in the journey ahead. We have tried our best to provide you with the tools towards self-actualization. The goal has not been to make you "mini-Azis" or "mini-Elliots." Rather we hope that we have given you the support, the community, and the mentoring to enable you to find your distinct voice as a cantor and as a rabbi.

Cantor Ellerin, by virtue of my vocal abilities (or lack thereof), I am forever one step removed from the music department. But what a joy it has been to see you lead our community. Whether you were conducting the Congregational Singers or working with our youth choir, I have admired your ability to draw out the song of every Jew with whom you work. The quality of your voice, the creativity and precision of your musicianship – you have led us so ably. Be it your *Ahavah rabbah* or *Birkat ha-ḥodesh* – staples of our synagogue and undoubtedly others – you have, in the best tradition of the cantorate, renewed classical compositions for a new generation.

Rabbi Loeterman, on more occasions than I can count, your leadership at Park Avenue Synagogue has drawn out Jewish souls no matter how hidden they may be: from the teens at the food pantry, bnei mitzvah students, families in a moment of loss, a classroom of students enraptured by your presence. Our community will not soon forget the Women's Network Shabbat last December, when you, in partnership with Cantor Lissek, prompted countless women to consider the mitzvah of *tallit*. It is not just that you are gifted with a distinctive voice of rabbinical leadership, but your rabbinical leadership has enabled so many of our community to find themselves in the tapestry of our tradition. And if you will allow me a moment of personal indulgence, in your presence I find myself seeking to be the best version of my own self, as a rabbi, mentor, and friend. For that, I will be ever grateful.

Both you, Cantor Ellerin, and you, Rabbi Loeterman, have impacted this community in ways we could not have imagined when you first entered our lives. We are so grateful to you for your leadership, but most importantly, for revealing to us the possibilities within us all. May you know only success in the coming chapters of your lives and may you always know the ongoing support of our community.

In the Torah reading of the week ahead, we will encounter the priestly blessing, the most ancient benediction on record for our people. It does, of course, call on God to bless us and be gracious unto us. But the radiance it bestows is not only external. It is a radiance that emanates from within, that sacred moment when God's image is brought into full relief in our countenance and in our deeds. Ben and Leah, Cantor Ellerin and Rabbi Loeterman, as we thank you, as we send you on your way, and as we bless you going forward, may the fullness of God's presence always shine forth, and may each of you, in your journey ahead, cause Torah to shine forth from all those lucky enough to be drawn into the circle of your embrace.

B'ha·alot'kha

The Best Defense

One year ago, in June of 2014, Park Avenue Synagogue hosted President Shimon Peres in his final farewell address to the American Jewish community. You may recall, as I do, our anxious questions as we awaited word on the fate of the three kidnapped Israeli teenagers – Naftali Fraenkel, Gilad Shaer, and Eyal Yifrach. And you, like me, can also recall our dashed hopes as their murdered bodies were found the very next day. On this, their first yahrzeits, we remember them and pray that the Fraenkel, Shaer, and Yifrach families will find comfort after an unspeakable loss.

One year later, we gather to celebrate Shabbat and welcome another great Israeli statesman, MK Yair Lapid, into our community. I cannot help but reflect on the year gone by. The kidnappings and murders, last summer's war with Gaza, the ongoing threat of a nuclear Iran, the emergence of new threats in a radicalized and destabilized Middle East. A world Jewry on edge after the attacks last summer in Sarcelles and last January in Paris. A virulent anti-Semitism which at worst has proven violent, and more often than not is a pernicious campaign to delegitimize Israel in the world community.

The year gone by has been testing and transformative for so many reasons. Israel has emerged with a right-leaning government that has found itself at odds with the American administration. This year will not be remembered as a strong one for United States-Israel relations. And we, the American Jewish community, have at times found ourselves squirming at the pinch of seeing the Israel we love so stand at odds with our American elected leadership.

We here in this synagogue, a proud Conservative/Masorti congregation, have been watching with increasing concern the tightening grip of the Chief Rabbinate in Israel on matters of personal identity. We see an Israel that does not recognize the Judaism that is preached and practiced here. An Israel that does not recognize the marriages or conversions of a non-Haredi rabbinate. An Israel in which a special needs bar mitzvah was canceled by the mayor of Rehovot last month. Why? For the sin of being celebrated under non-Orthodox auspices. At times, at too many times, we have been left to wonder whether Israel loves us as much as we love Israel. For Israel, for the diaspora-Israel relationship, the year has been a difficult one and we do ourselves, Israel, and our relationship a disservice if we try to sweep these difficulties under the rug.

So as we reflect on this year, as we prepare for our summers, as I introduce our guest, what is the message for this day? To you *Ḥaver Knesset* Yair Lapid, Chairman of the Yesh Atid Party, it is an easy task. I have but two words for you: Thank you. Or better yet, in Hebrew: *Todah rabbah*. Thank you for being an advocate on behalf of Israel. Thank you for taking a stand on the internal and external threats pulling at the fabric of Israeli society. Thank you for being at the forefront of the effort to create a pluralistic vision of Jewish life in Israel. Thank you for speaking out whenever the sinister head of BDS rears itself in Europe, America, or anywhere else. Most of all, *todah rabbah* for being the strongest voice on record for Jewish peoplehood in the Knesset, a spokesperson for *arevut*, global Jewish responsibility. Though we live here, and you live in Israel, we know – because you have taught us – "I could be you and you could be me." It is a realization that alerts us to our common past, our present mutual obligations, and our shared Jewish future. *Mei-omek libi u-v'shem kulanu*, from the depths of my heart and in the name of all of us: *Todah rabbah*.

And to you, my Park Avenue Synagogue family, when it comes to the challenges of the hour, I have but one message, as taught by a great American, Vince Lombardi: "The best defense is a great offense." What I mean by this is that we have a choice. We can sit here and *schrei gevalt*, complaining about the American administration, the Israeli government, the Chief Rabbinate, and the diaspora-Israel relationship, or we can actually do something about it. We at Park Avenue Synagogue can stand as a model of what it means to love Israel, to advocate on her behalf publicly and privately, to defend her against existential threats, and to represent the "sane center" that is so desperately needed in our public discourse. We can show the world that one can advocate for Israel's security and for a two-state solution at one and the same time. That we need not and will not yield an inch to those who would jeopardize either Israel's democratic or Jewish character, on the right or the left. On those matters most dear to us, that sit at the heart of the promise of Israel, we can and must respond in word and in deed.

And yes, as a Conservative/Masorti congregation, we must work towards the day that the Judaism we love so has a home in Israel. But this message is made most clearly not by playing defense, not by complaining, but by living vibrant and engaged Jewish lives, by building dynamic Jewish communities that dare not be ignored. There are those in Israel who believe that American Jewry is a passing fad; why take us seriously, they say, when we won't be here in another generation. If we want – if you want – Israel to take your Judaism seriously, we ourselves need to take our own Judaism seriously. In other words, we need to play offense. We need every member of Knesset visiting America to see dynamic non-Orthodox communities like ours, living engaged Jewish lives, committed to the Jewish people, committed to the well-being of Israel. The force of our argument will never come by way of complaining at a distance. A Jewish identity whose foundation is built on vicarious complaints about the Israeli Rabbinate is not a Judaism that will last or is worth defending in the first place. Our Torah reading recounts that when Moses was approached by Joshua regarding two men – Eldad and Medad – who claimed to speak on behalf of God, Moses reproached not the two men, but Joshua, "Would that all the people speak for God." In other words, take your own yiddishkeit seriously, and people will take you seriously.

Haver Knesset Yair Lapid, on this visit, and on all future visits to America, please know that you have a home with us at Park Avenue Synagogue. Come in peace and return in peace. Return to Israel with the message that you saw a vibrant, pluralistic, non-Orthodox, community that loves Israel and stands by Israel. Like two strings on a violin, though separated by a distance, when touched by a bow, we have but one voice. That is my message to you, and that is my message to my community.

Please join me in welcoming *Ḥaver Knesset* Yair Lapid.

Four Cups of Freedom

5775/2015

A Haggadah Supplement
On the Occasion of the 150th Anniversary
of the End of the American Civil War

Hag Pesah sameah!

You have seen what I did to the Egyptians, how I
bore you on eagles' wings and brought you to Me.

Exodus 19:4

Four Cups of Freedom: On the Occasion of the 150th Anniversary of the End of the Civil War

T his year Pesah coincides with the sesquicentennial of the end of the American Civil War. As we turn our attention to retelling ancient Israel's journey to freedom, we are struck by how the narrative that has sustained the Jewish people for millennia resonates in the story of our country.

The Biblical struggle for freedom was a touchstone in the founding of America, in African-American spirituals, in the Civil Rights movement of the twentieth century, and beyond. In 1776 Benjamin Franklin and Thomas Jefferson proposed the image on the cover of this supplement for the Great Seal of United States. It shows Moses leading the Israelites in celebration as the waters of the Red Sea engulf the Egyptians. As citizens of a nation founded on the principle of freedom for all, we find the Passover story in both our Jewish and American narratives: the journey from slavery to freedom, from oppression to redemption, from the wilderness to nationhood. The story of Passover is a bridge between our identities as Jews and as Americans.

The word Haggadah literally means "telling." As you tell the story of Passover at your Seder, we invite you to use this Haggadah companion to simultaneously tell the story of America. Following the order of the Seder, this supplement provides texts from American history to read and discuss at specific points in the Haggadah. Use just one or use them all! We hope that these selections will bring lively discussion and debate to your Seder, allowing you to experience the story of Passover in a new way.

Rabbi Elliot J. Cosgrove
Leah Loeterman, Rabbinic Intern

To accompany *Yahatz*
(breaking the middle matzah)

Thomas Jefferson, *Declaration of Independence*
July 4, 1776

We hold these truths to be self-evident, that all men are created equal, that they are endowed by their Creator with certain unalienable Rights, that among these are Life, Liberty and the pursuit of Happiness. — That to secure these rights, Governments are instituted among Men, deriving their just powers from the consent of the governed, — That whenever any Form of Government becomes destructive of these ends, it is the Right of the People to alter or to abolish it, and to institute new Government, laying its foundation on such principles and organizing its powers in such form, as to them shall seem most likely to effect their Safety and Happiness. Prudence, indeed, will dictate that Governments long established should not be changed for light and transient causes; and accordingly all experience hath shewn, that mankind are more disposed to suffer, while evils are sufferable, than to right themselves by abolishing the forms to which they are accustomed. But when a long train of abuses and usurpations, pursuing invariably the same Object evinces a design to reduce them under absolute Despotism, it is their right, it is their duty, to throw off such Government, and to provide new Guards for their future security. — Such has been the patient sufferance of these Colonies; and such is now the necessity which constrains them to alter their former Systems of Government. The history of the present King of Great Britain is a history of repeated injuries and usurpations, all having in direct object the establishment of an absolute Tyranny over these States.

Commentary

During the *Yahatz* portion of the Seder, we break the middle matzah in half and put away one half to eat later as the afikoman. In doing so, we are reminded that a journey to freedom also involves a break with the past. Like Moses before him, Jefferson understood that the founding of our nation was both the fulfillment of an ideal and a painful separation from Britain. Breaks are not always clean, though they may be necessary. Breaking takes courage.

For all Jefferson's idealism, we must confront the fact that he himself was a slave owner. Despite articulating a vision of the "consent of the governed," he harbored a blind spot to that very vision. We continue to wrestle with this inner contradiction of our founding fathers.

Questions for Discussion

- Which is harder for a leader to do: provide a vision for the future or declare a break with the past?

- How do you reconcile the inherent contradiction upon which our country was founded: that America is to be a nation of free people, yet some of its founders owned slaves?

To accompany *Mah Nishtanah*
(Four Questions)

**Elizabeth Cady Stanton, Seneca Falls Convention
July 19, 1848**

But we are assembled to protest against a form of government existing
without the consent of the governed – to declare our right to be free as
man is free, to be represented in the government which we are taxed to
support, to have such is graceful laws as give man the power to chastise
and imprison his wife, to take the wages which she earns, the property
which she inherits, and, in case of separation, the children of her love; laws
which make her the mere dependent on his bounty. It is to protest against
such unjust laws as these that we are assembled today, and to have them,
if possible, forever erased from our statute books, deeming them a shame
and a disgrace to a Christian republic in the nineteenth century. We have
met to uplift woman's fallen divinity upon an even pedestal with man's.
And, strange as it may seem to many, we now demand our right to vote
according to the declaration of the government under which we live.

6 • Four Cups of Freedom: On the Occasion of the 150th Anniversary of the End of the Civil War

This right no one pretends to deny. We need not prove ourselves equal to Daniel Webster to enjoy this privilege, for the ignorant Irishman in the ditch has all the civil rights he has. We need not prove our muscular power equal to this same Irishman to enjoy this privilege, for the most tiny, weak, ill-shaped stripling of twenty-one has all the civil rights of the Irishman. We have no objection to discuss the question of equality, for we feel that the weight of argument lies wholly with us, but we wish the question of equality kept distinct from the question of rights, for the proof of the one does not determine the truth of the other. All white men in this country have the same rights, however they may differ in mind, body, or estate.

Commentary

Seneca Falls was America's first women's rights convention, at which Stanton made an impassioned case for women's suffrage. For Stanton, the question of rights is the foundational question from which all others follow. Stanton challenges the existing order, questioning the fact that women cannot enjoy the same rights that men enjoy in America, the country that champions freedom and "the consent of the governed." She implores her audience and the larger public to keep "the question of equality ... distinct from the question of rights, for the proof of the one does not determine the truth of the other." Stanton adopts the inclusive language of the Declaration of Independence to make the case for women's right to vote. Stanton's battle was eventually won after her lifetime, with the adoption of the 19th Amendment in 1920.

Questions for Discussion

- What are the explicit and the hidden ways by which people are disenfranchised? Who remains disenfranchised today?

- What tasks remain towards fulfilling Stanton's vision of women's equality?

To be sung with *Avadim Hayinu*
(We Were Slaves)

Go Down Moses

When Israel was in Egypt's land,
Let my people go,
Oppressed so hard they could not stand,
Let my people go.
Go down, Moses,
Way down in Egypt's land,
Tell old Pharaoh,
Let my people go.

Commentary

"Go Down, Moses" was an African-American slaves' song, or spiritual, popular during the 1800s. Slaves would often use spirituals as ways to remember and communicate, as well as to provide a rhythm for repetitive manual work. "Go Down, Moses" was one of the spirituals that Harriet Tubman used as a code in the Underground Railroad with slaves fleeing Maryland, to let them know that there was danger and it was not safe to come out.

We spend much of the Passover Seder fulfilling the mitzvah of retelling the story of the Israelites' exodus from Egypt, the journey from slavery to freedom, often through songs such as *Avadim Hayinu*, which similarly tells the story of the Israelites' being slaves in Egypt under Pharaoh.

Although Moses figures prominently in this particular spiritual, he is never mentioned by name in the Haggadah itself, despite being the hero and leader of the story. We are to remember that it was God who performed the miracles in Egypt, at the banks of the Red Sea, and in the wilderness; it was God who delivered us from slavery to freedom, not a human.

Questions for Discussion

- Passover calls on us to empathize with the suffering of others. How can we prioritize our own communal needs while remaining responsive to the injustices of the world at large?

- Is it justified to keep Moses' name out of the Haggadah? What lessons of leadership can we learn from this striking omission?

To accompany the Second of the Four Children

**Frederick Douglass, "The Meaning of July Fourth for the Negro"
July 5, 1852**

Fellow-citizens, pardon me, allow me to ask, why am I called upon to speak here to-day? What have I, or those I represent, to do with your national independence? Are the great principles of political freedom and of natural justice, embodied in that Declaration of Independence, extended to us? I am not included within the pale of this glorious anniversary! Your high independence only reveals the immeasurable distance between us. The rich inheritance of justice, liberty, prosperity and independence, bequeathed by your fathers, is shared by you, not by me. The sunlight that brought light and healing to you, has brought stripes and death to me. This Fourth July is yours, not mine. You may rejoice, I must mourn. To drag a man in fetters into the grand illuminated temple of liberty, and call upon him to join you in joyous anthems, were inhuman mockery and sacrilegious irony. Do you mean, citizens, to mock me, by asking me to speak to-day? If so, there is a parallel to your conduct. And let me warn you that it is dangerous to copy the example of a nation whose crimes, towering up to heaven, were thrown down by the breath of the Almighty, burying that nation in irrevocable ruin!

Fellow-citizens, above your national, tumultuous joy, I hear the mournful wail of millions! whose chains, heavy and grievous yesterday, are, to-day, rendered more intolerable by the jubilee shouts that reach them. If I do forget, if I do not faithfully remember those bleeding children of sorrow this day, "may my right hand forget her cunning, and may my tongue cleave to the roof of my mouth!" To forget them, to pass lightly over their wrongs, and to chime in with the popular theme, would be treason most scandalous and shocking, and would make me a reproach before God and the world.... I do not hesitate to declare, with all my soul, that the character and conduct of this nation never looked blacker to me than on this 4th of July!

Commentary

The Haggadah harshly rebukes the "wicked" child for removing himself from the central narrative of our people when he asks "What is this service to *you*?" Douglass uses similar language in this speech, proclaiming "This Fourth of July is yours, not mine." Throughout the speech, Douglass uses almost exclusively "you" language, thereby removing himself – and by extension all African-Americans – from the celebration of the holiday devoted to the birth of the nation. Douglass feels compelled to remove himself from the holiday celebrations because he cannot celebrate a nation that claims to stand for freedom, yet still allows slavery and brutal oppression of his people.

Questions for Discussion

Is "wicked" the right name for this child? "Rebellious?" What would you call this child?

The second child feels left out of the Passover celebration, and Douglass feels on the outside of the July 4th celebration. Who else in our society is left out?

To accompany the Ten Plagues

**President Abraham Lincoln's Second Inaugural Address
March 4, 1865**

Neither party expected for the war the magnitude or the duration which it has already attained. Neither anticipated that the cause of the conflict might cease with or even before the conflict itself should cease. Each looked for an easier triumph, and a result less fundamental and astounding. Both read the same Bible and pray to the same God, and each invokes His aid against the other. It may seem strange that any men should dare to ask a just God's assistance in wringing their bread from the sweat of other men's faces, but let us judge not, that we be not judged. The prayers of both could not be answered. That of neither has been answered fully. The Almighty has His own purposes. "Woe unto the world because of offenses; for it must needs be that offenses come, but woe to that man by whom the offense cometh." If we shall suppose that American slavery is one of those offenses which, in the providence of God, must needs come, but which, having continued through His appointed time, He now wills to remove, and that He gives to both North and South this terrible war as the woe due to those by whom the offense came, shall we discern therein any departure from those divine attributes which the believers in a living God always ascribe to Him? Fondly do we hope, fervently do we pray, that this mighty scourge of war may speedily pass away. Yet, if God wills that it continue until all the wealth piled by the bondsman's two hundred and fifty years of unrequited toil shall be sunk, and until every drop of blood drawn with the lash shall be paid by another drawn with the sword, as was said three thousand years ago, so still it must be said "the judgements of the Lord are true and righteous altogether."

With malice toward none, with charity for all, with firmness in the right as God gives us to see the right, let us strive on to finish the work we are in, to bind up the nation's wounds, to care for him who shall have borne the battle and for his widow and his orphan, to do all which may achieve and cherish a just and lasting peace among ourselves and with all nations.

Commentary

The enduring poetry of Lincoln's Second Inaugural is his ability to acknowledge both sides of the conflict. Lincoln, the leader of the North, recognizes the blood and sacrifices made by people of both North and South. So too, as we recall the Ten Plagues, we celebrate God's wondrous miracles, but also spill out a drop of wine from our cups for every plague recited – an acknowledgement of loss of life on the other side. The Egyptians too were God's creatures.

Questions for Discussion

- Pick a controversial social issue about which you are passionate. Can you provide a reasoned defense of the opposing side?

- The Egyptians brutally oppressed the Israelites in Egypt. Should we even acknowledge that they lost their lives?

To be read after singing *Dayenu*

Reverend Dr. Martin Luther King, Jr., "I Have a Dream"
August 28, 1963

There are those who are asking the devotees of civil rights, "When will you be satisfied?" We can never be satisfied as long as the Negro is the victim of the unspeakable horrors of police brutality. We can never be satisfied as long as our bodies, heavy with the fatigue of travel, cannot gain lodging in the motels of the highways and the hotels of the cities. We cannot be satisfied as long as the Negro's basic mobility is from a smaller ghetto to a larger one. We can never be satisfied as long as our children are stripped of their self-hood and robbed of their dignity by signs stating: "For Whites Only." We cannot be satisfied as long as a Negro in Mississippi cannot vote and a Negro in New York believes he has nothing for which to vote. No, no, we are not satisfied, and we will not be satisfied until "justice rolls down like waters, and righteousness like a mighty stream."

132

I am not unmindful that some of you have come here out of great trials and tribulations. Some of you have come fresh from narrow jail cells. And some of you have come from areas where your quest – quest for freedom left you battered by the storms of persecution and staggered by the winds of police brutality. You have been the veterans of creative suffering. Continue to work with the faith that unearned suffering is redemptive. Go back to Mississippi, go back to Alabama, go back to South Carolina, go back to Georgia, go back to Louisiana, go back to the slums and ghettos of our northern cities, knowing that somehow this situation can and will be changed.

Commentary

Dayenu is one of the most popular and lively songs at the Seder. *Dayenu! It would have been enough!* We recognize the magnitude of God's work, and we would have been grateful and satisfied with each step alone. King, however, calls on us to "never to be satisfied" as long as injustice still exists. Both King's words and the words of *Dayenu* are essential texts, but reflect very different religious and social-political sensibilities.

Questions for Discussion

◦ Do you think King would have ever said "*Dayenu*"? In what circumstance?

◦ In our contemporary marches to freedom, when should we say "*Dayenu*," or should we "never be satisfied"? Why?

To accompany *B'khol Dor Va-dor*
(In Every Generation)

**President Abraham Lincoln, "Gettysburg Address"
November 19, 1863**

Four score and seven years ago our fathers brought forth, on this continent, a new nation, conceived in Liberty, and dedicated to the proposition that all men are created equal. Now we are engaged in a great civil war, testing whether that nation, or any nation so conceived and so dedicated, can long endure. We are met on a great battlefield of that war. We have come to dedicate a portion of that field, as a final resting place for those who here gave their lives that that nation might live. It is altogether fitting and proper that we should do this. But, in a larger sense, we cannot dedicate—we cannot consecrate—we cannot hallow—this ground. The brave men, living and dead, who struggled here, have consecrated it, far above our poor power to add or detract. The world will little note, nor long remember what we say here, but it can never forget what they did here. It is for us the living, rather, to be dedicated here to the unfinished work which they who fought here have thus far so nobly advanced. It is rather for us to be here dedicated to the great task remaining before us—that from these honored dead we take increased devotion to that cause for which they here gave the last full measure of devotion—that we here highly resolve that these dead shall not have died in vain—that this nation, under God, shall have a new birth of freedom—and that government of the people, by the people, for the people, shall not perish from the earth.

Commentary

The Haggadah instructs us: *B'khol dor va-dor hayav adam lir'ot et atzmo k'ilu hu yatza mi-mitzrayim.* In every generation, we are all obligated to see ourselves as though we personally emerged from Egypt and are thus charged to continue the work of past generations. Likewise, Lincoln calls on his listeners to continue their work so that "that these dead shall not die in vain." In every generation, we must commit ourselves to fulfill the legacies of those who came before.

Questions for Discussion

- Which is better: to choose your own causes or to adopt those of prior generations? What causes are you committed to that reflect the values and commitments of a past generation?

- Do you think Lincoln would understand the present civil rights struggles as a continuation of the "unfinished work" of those who gave their lives at Gettysburg? Do you?

To be read before opening the door for *Eliyahu HaNavi*, Elijah the Prophet

Rabbi Abraham Joshua Heschel, "The Religious Basis of Equality of Opportunity: the Segregation of God"
1963

At the first conference on religion and race, the main participants were Pharaoh and Moses. Moses' words were: "Thus says the Lord, the God of Israel, let My people go that they may celebrate a feast to Me." While Pharaoh retorted: "Who is the Lord, that I should heed this voice and let Israel go? I do not know the Lord, and moreover I will not let Israel go."

The outcome of that summit meeting has not come to an end. Pharaoh is not ready to capitulate. The exodus began, but is far from having been completed. In fact, it was easier for the children of Israel to cross the Red Sea than for a Negro to cross certain university campuses. ...

What we must do is to set an example, not merely to acknowledge the

Negro but to welcome him, not grudgingly but joyously, to take delight in enabling him to enjoy what is due to him. We are all *Pharaohs* or *slaves of Pharaohs*. It is sad to be a slave of Pharaoh. *It is horrible to be a Pharaoh.*

Daily we should take account and ask: What have I done today *to alleviate the anguish, to mitigate the evil, to prevent humiliation?*

Let there be a grain of prophet in every man!

Commentary

As we open the door for Elijah, we invite the prophetic voice into our home. Heschel, a prophet in his day, hopes for "a grain of a prophet in every man." Having lost most of his family in the Holocaust, Heschel spoke out against the injustices of his time. Heschel did not wait for a prophet, nor did he believe prophecy was the possession of any one individual. Rather, he wanted everyone to do the sacred work of repair and justice and to join the struggle for freedom.

Questions for Discussion

- Complete your own version of Heschel's sentence: "It was easier for the children of Israel to cross the Red Sea than for ..."

- Answer Heschel's question: "What have I done today *to alleviate the anguish, to mitigate the evil, to prevent humiliation?*"

To accompany *Hallel*

**President Franklin Delano Roosevelt, "Four Freedoms" State of
the Union Address
January 6, 1941**

In the future days, which we seek to make secure, we look forward to a
world founded upon four essential human freedoms. The first is freedom
of speech and expression—everywhere in the world. The second is
freedom of every person to worship God in his own way—everywhere in
the world. The third is freedom from want—which, translated into world
terms, means economic understandings which will secure to every nation
a healthy peacetime life for its inhabitants everywhere in the world. The
fourth is freedom from fear—which, translated into world terms, means
a world-wide reduction of armaments to such a point and in such a
thorough fashion that no nation will be in a position to commit an act of
physical aggression against any neighbor—anywhere in the world. That is
no vision of a distant millennium. It is a definite basis for a kind of world

attainable in our own time and generation. ... The world order which we seek is the cooperation of free countries, working together in a friendly, civilized society. This nation has placed its destiny in the hands and heads and hearts of its millions of free men and women; and its faith in freedom under the guidance of God. Freedom means the supremacy of human rights everywhere. Our support goes to those who struggle to gain those rights or keep them. Our strength is our unity of purpose. To that high concept there can be no end save victory.

Commentary

With this address, Roosevelt first announced his decision to become involved in World War II, and to help the United States' allies already engaged in the war. His "Four Freedoms" were eventually incorporated into the United Nations' Universal Declaration of Human Rights.

The number four is repeated throughout the Haggadah: four cups of wine, four children, four questions. Each one of the four in these categories carries its own significance, but each one only works within the complete structure of the whole. Each cup of wine represents a redemptive act of freedom that God performed for the Israelites (Exodus 6:6-7). Roosevelt's "Four Freedoms" are significant individually; together they create a basic code of human rights and give expression to a redemptive vision for humankind.

Questions for Discussion

- Why do you think Roosevelt chose these four particular freedoms?

- If you had to make a new list of "four freedoms," what would they be? What would you add to or replace on Roosevelt's list?

To be read at *Nirtzah*, the conclusion of the Seder

President Barack Obama, Speech in Selma, Alabama on the 50th Anniversary of the March from Selma to Montgomery
March 7, 2015

Fifty years from Bloody Sunday, our march is not yet finished. But we are getting closer. Two hundred and thirty-nine years after this nation's founding, our union is not yet perfect. But we are getting closer. Our job's easier because somebody already got us through that first mile. Somebody already got us over that bridge. When it feels the road's too hard, when the torch we've been passed feels too heavy, we will remember these early travelers, and draw strength from their example, and hold firmly the words of the prophet Isaiah: "Those who hope in the Lord will renew their strength. They will soar on wings like eagles. They will run and not grow weary. They will walk and not be faint."

We honor those who walked so we could run. We must run so our children soar. And we will not grow weary. For we believe in the power of an awesome God, and we believe in this country's sacred promise. May He bless those warriors of justice no longer with us, and bless the United States of America.

Commentary

The conclusion of the Seder is *Nirtzah*, in which we proclaim *L'shanah ha-ba'ah birushalayim!* Next year in Jerusalem! Our Seder ends on a note of hope: just as our ancestors survived generations of slavery in Egypt and were freed, so too we look forward to freedom, and the ultimate redemption. However, there is an internal paradox as we end the Seder: *Nirtzah* signals the end of the seder, but "next year in Jerusalem" implies that there is something more to strive for, something larger to work for, an end goal that has not yet been attained.

In his remarks in Selma recently, Obama reflected on the struggles for freedom in America, and similarly looked toward hope and toward the future as we partner with those who came before: "our march is not yet finished. But we are getting closer." We are one step closer to Jerusalem, *L'shanah ha-ba'ah*, next year, we will be there!

Questions for Discussion

- Is the march for freedom ever complete? Do we ever reach the Promised Land?

- Go around the table: Make a concrete commitment that you can return to next year to take the next step in bettering God's world.

Park Avenue Synagogue

Park Avenue Synagogue – *Agudat Yesharim*, the Association of the Righteous – was founded in 1882. From modest beginnings, it has grown into the flagship congregation of the Conservative movement.

In 1882 a group of German-speaking Jews founded a congregation and named it Temple Gates of Hope. They converted a church building at 115 East 86th Street into a synagogue and soon the new congregation was known as the Eighty-Sixth Street Temple. Some twelve years after its founding, the synagogue joined together with Congregation Agudat Yesharim, which gave the congregation its Hebrew name, which appears on the cornerstone of the Rita and George M. Shapiro House at the corner of Madison Avenue and 87th Street. In this congregation the sermons were still preached in German. More amalgamations were to come. A nearby synagogue, the Seventy-Second Street Temple – itself a product of the earlier merger of Beth Israel and Bikkur Cholim, two congregations that had their beginnings on the Lower East Side in the 1840s and moved uptown to Lexington Avenue and 72nd Street in 1920 – merged with the Eighty-Sixth Street Temple/Agudat Yesharim.

In 1923 the Eighty-Sixth Street Temple petitioned the State of New York to change its name to Park Avenue Synagogue. A new sanctuary was constructed on 87th Street three years later and dedicated in March 1927. This building remains the present-day sanctuary. In 1928 the last of the mergers took place when Atereth Israel, a congregation of Alsatian Jews who worshipped in their building on East 82nd Street, added their strength to the Park Avenue Synagogue.

Designed by architect Walter Schneider in 1926, the synagogue building is one of the last synagogues to have been built in the Moorish style, which first became popular in the 1850s in Europe. It features one of the most beautiful cast stone façades in New York and a hand-painted bimah. Moorish decoration is used throughout the interior of the sanctuary, from Arabesque dadoes to the design for the domed ceiling.

In 1954 a new building was dedicated in memory of Rabbi Milton Steinberg, who had come to the Park Avenue Synagogue in 1933. It was designed by Kelly and Gruzen with architect Robert Greenstein (a Park Avenue Synagogue congregant and former student of Le Corbusier). The renowned American artist Adolph Gottlieb was commissioned to design its stained glass curtain wall façade, the largest continuous expanse of stained glass of its time. Gottlieb's images were intended to reflect Rabbi Steinberg's teachings, which advocated the integration of traditional Jewish practice within modernity and American experience.

In 1980 this building was incorporated into the Rita and George M. Shapiro House, housing the educational facilities of the synagogue. It features a distinctive rusticated façade of Mankato limestone, the color of Jerusalem stone when fully matured, and was designed by Bassuk Panero & Zelnick architects and modified by Schuman, Lichenstein, Calman & Efron with the assistance of James Rush Jarrett and Dean Bernard Spring of the School of Architecture at City University.

Prominently displayed on its façade are two bronze sculptures by Nathan Rapoport, "Tragedy and Triumph." The lower bas relief depicts Dr. Janusz Korczak surrounded by the children of his orphanage in Warsaw as they were deported to their death at Treblinka. The upper panel depicts three Israelis – a pioneer, a soldier, and an older man – carrying back to Israel the Menorah that was removed from the Temple by Titus and the Romans during the destruction of Jerusalem. The inscribed dedication reads: "To the sacred memory of the million Jewish children who perished in the Holocaust." Above the dedication is the Hebrew word *Zakhor* – Remember. Dedicated as a living memorial to the Holocaust, this building expresses Park Avenue Synagogue's hope that the memory of these children will inspire new generations of educated and proud Jews and ensure the continuity of Jewish tradition, history, faith, and heritage.

Park Avenue Synagogue
Board of Trustees, Clergy & Staff, 2015–2016